PROCESS DESIGN for HUMAN RESOURCES

VINCENT TUCKWOOD

> There's a trick to making things work in HR. In fact, there are a few. Full of practical insights gleaned from real-world experience, this book nails it. If you want to get things done in Human Resources, this is how to do it."

Laurie Ruettimann
Author & HR Consultant

> Vince has a unique ability to bring a broad, creative and strategic perspective to situations while also being grounded in reality and help with what needs to be done in the short term. It's a wonderful balance to have in a consulting partner. I worked with Vince at Pfizer and then at my next company asked him in to help with talent strategy and analytics work. He is very adept at HR transformation work, because he's been there and led it. He approaches his work with great collaboration, compassion and flexibility."

Wendy Branche
SVP & CTO

> *Vince is a passionate leader who has visionary ideas that inspire and motivate a team to achieve a common mission. He is a talented communicator who is personable and down-to-earth, with an immense sense of humor. I consider myself fortunate for the opportunity to be have been a part of his team.*

Jeri Molintas McGonnell
Program & Product Director

> *I began to work with Vince in the spring of 2003 on a global HR service delivery initiative for Pfizer. Vince is honestly strategic, deeply committed and a professional who believes that teams create the best outcomes."*

Kristina DiPalo
Professional Coach & Communications Strategist, Elysian Communications

> Vince is visionary. He is incredibly intelligent and capable of looking across the breadth of the HR function and determining at the macro level what long- and short-term strategic changes can be made to better meet the needs of the business.
>
> He is extremely capable using current and emerging technologies to better align the delivery of HR services and consultation across the function.
>
> Vince is a tremendous talent and I will not be surprised to see him recognized by external HR experts as one of the finest transformational thinkers within the HR function."

Michele McCormick CIR, CDR
Talent Acquisition Expert

PROCESS DESIGN for HUMAN RESOURCES

VINCENT TUCKWOOD

PROCESS DESIGN FOR HUMAN RESOURCES
The right WAY to make things FLOW in HR

Copyright © 2022 Vincent Tuckwood

All rights reserved. No part of this book may be used or reproduced by any means, graphic, electronic, or mechanical, including photocopying, recording, taping or by any information storage retrieval system without the written permission of the publisher except in the case of brief quotations embodied in critical articles and reviews.

Because of the dynamic nature of the Internet, any Web addresses or links contained in this book may have changed since publication and may no longer be valid. The views expressed in this work are solely those of the author and do not necessarily reflect the views of the publisher, and the publisher hereby disclaims any responsibility for them.

Published by:

View Beyond LLC
20 Maple Terrace
Waterford
CT 06385
USA

ISBN: 9798362162566

FOREWORD 13

WHY DESIGN YOUR PROCESS? 19
- The best practice myth 23
- Who's involved… And why? 25
- A couple of (pretty safe) assumptions 26
- The system made me do it… 29

PROCESS DESIGN BASICS 33
- What is a process? 33
- Approaches to Process Design 33
- The basic building blocks of Process Design 34
- What is Process Design? 36

LAYING THE GROUNDWORK 39
- For the sake of what (and who)? 40
- Fit-for-purpose processes 50
- A Strong Foundation 54
- The critical importance of sponsorship 57
- Managing the (sometimes hostile) landscape 70
- Getting the plane off-the-ground 78

DESIGNING THE PROCESS 79
- WHY we are doing the process 81
- WHAT happens during this process? 90
- WHO is involved in the process? 99
- HOW the process works 112

REFINING THE PROCESS 129
- Subject Matter Experts 130
- Functional Intersections & Dependencies 139
- Exception Handling 145

TOWARDS IMPLEMENTATION 155
- People 156
- Translating your process pack 159
- Sharing the wiring 167

BEYOND IMPLEMENTATION 169
- Change Control 170
- Some quick thoughts on shadow systems 174
- A final thought on process design 176

WHAT HAPPENS NEXT? 179

FOREWORD

To say I was surprised by the positive reception to my previous book, *Project Management For Human Resources*, would be a significant understatement. I did, after all write it partly as an antidote for being locked down in the early stages of the COVID-19 pandemic; not exactly a boredom cure, but definitely a way of staying centered and sane during the quiet upheaval.

PM4HR - as I know it, because it's such a long title to type out! - was published in late-May 2020 and, almost straight out of the gate, found an audience who a) understood that there's a better way to get things done in HR; and b) were relieved to find that there was at least one like-mind elsewhere in the profession who is unwilling to accept the stodgy *status quo*

(Actually, as I've learned, there are many of us!)

To a person, everyone who has reached out to me having read the book has asked me how I knew what was going on in their own little corner of HR-world.

The answer, I must admit, is not magical in nature - any insight I have has been hard-earned and, as I often say, I have the battle scars to prove it!

The most humbling question though and one I did not expect to hear, let alone multiple times, was *"what's next?"*

If project management is the HOW of getting work done in HR, then the obvious answer to the question is the WHAT of the work we do. Now, that could, and will, span multiple books because, well, we do a LOT, but I've chosen to focus upon process design as the first area.

Why so?

Well, at some level nearly everything we do rests upon a process. Everything.

And yet we aren't known as masters of process - in fact, it's weird to me that it's still an uphill struggle to even suggest process-based continuous improvement to HR - if anything, we're known for the complete opposite.

And, within our function, process design is typically delegated off to someone in the operations or administrative group, and viewed as *"beneath REAL HR pros"*.

What BS!

Our function has an almost-willful blind spot, refusing to notice, admit or accept that process is at the core of our value-add; it's well past time we brought it center-stage.

But in order to do that, in our first chapter together, we're going to ask a painful yet revealing question: WHY DOES HR SUCK?

A PROCESS IS A CONSISTENT, REPEATABLE SERIES OF STEPS TOWARDS A CLEARLY-DEFINED END-POINT

WHY DESIGN YOUR PROCESS?

What would you say if I asked you a simple question:

"WHY DOES HR SUCK?"

Chances are that everyone, and I mean everyone, has their own opinion - and they're more than likely very open to sharing it with you. Loudly.

You may vociferously agree, or you may drop into knee-jerk defensiveness or any other number of reactions. You may even be intrigued by the question and eager to seek more data.

But, before you run off and create a multi-variate feedback survey, I took the liberty of doing a quick bit of research.

I asked that question of Google; it wasn't a pleasant experience.

In fact, I encourage you to do the same, then read at least the first page of articles and discussion threads that come up. It's painful feedback, and not always constructive in nature, nor polite in language; even the most rose-tinted summary of the research would indicate that people are experiencing some level of negative emotion *as a result* of our activities.

Yet, even though many of the articles and comments are firmly rooted in emotional substance, in the main these are not the rants of aggrieved know-nothings that we might label as *"whiners"*, or contest that we *"can't please all of the people all of the time…"*

The criticism is often eloquent, and clearly grounded in lived-experience and, given this, we have to ask what's giving rise to this reaction? Where do people experience, and therefore *feel*, the activity of Human Resources.

To dig deeper, I aggregated the content of the first page of my search into tagcrowd.com - and, after removing some obvious repeats (*"Human"*, *"Resources"*, *"HR"*, *"Business"*, etc.), here's what turned up:

ago benefits **best** create customer
department function **hiring** important
job needs office **organization**
performance person problem
process professionals really
recruiting report share strategic **strategy** talent
things think top understand **work**

From this, it's not too big of a leap to assert that process is really important to perceptions of our function's effectiveness, efficiency and value.

Through a slightly different lens, this word cloud may be saying that, while thought leaders in HR, Talent & Organization Development love to talk about strategic HR, talent and workforce planning, organization culture, and all the other sexy stuff that sells conference seats, we are more often judged on how our process helps people get work done - with particular emphasis on hiring and performance.

That may be reading too much into a word cloud that literally took me no more than a few minutes to put together - it's hardly what I would call grounded research...

Or, it may be that the issue is staring us right in the face and is so simple that it can be found with such little digging.

PROCESS UNDERPINS THE VAST MAJORITY OF WHAT HR DELIVERS... SO PROCESS COUNTS

And yet, even a quick review of the majority of HR functions, in organizations of all sizes and shapes, will show processes that have evolved over time, warping and adapting, replete with *hand-me-down* customization and bureaucratic caveats.

Those processes will have flexed to allow for customizations and outliers, sometimes forcing newly-acquired, simple software solutions to adopt burdensome filters and rule-sets, backed up by paper-based data handling, and managed by subject matter gate-keepers.

In reality, most HR processes are *anything but* designed.

I'm sorry if this sounds harsh but… well, it needs to be because I need you to listen; we can't hope to fix something if we're in avoidance/denial of just how broken it is.

And HR's dogmatic allegiance to *"the way things are done around here"* means that we don't even ask the question that counts the most:

IS THIS PROCESS EVEN NECESSARY?

Take a process that has been gaining much attention in the past couple of years: *Performance Management*.

Of course, managing performance has always been a thing but, as the capability of electronic storage and transmission of performance data became more readily available, so the process of Performance Management gained its capital-letter status and grew into the often cumbersome beast it is today.

The spread of Performance Management as a standalone process really gained momentum during the 1990s and, by the 2000s, it was *de rigeur* (and often coupled with development planning to boot!)

More recently - and, indeed in one of the articles that contributed to the word-cloud above - the annual Performance Management process has been called into question, and a leading edge of companies have already left it in the rear-view mirror.

Now, given that the Performance Management process has been, and continues to be, a thing, let me ask…

When did you last design your Performance Management process?

Maybe it was recently, or maybe not, but that question leads to another…

Did you really *design* the process, or just change some stuff that was already there?

In most cases, I'm willing to bet the latter is the case, precisely because that's how the majority of HR processes have come to be in their current state:

OUR PROCESSES ARE LARGELY ITERATIONS OF WHAT'S GONE BEFORE

It is, after all, the path of least resistance in the vast majority of situations. And it's very much easier to tinker around the edges than it is to root-and-branch the whole thing.

But there's a couple of things at play in this denial/avoidance of process design; much more insidious aspects of HR organizational culture and norms.

The best practice myth

Firstly, I'll declare an opinion. I'm no fan of the term *"best practice"*.

I love great things, done elegantly, but I see the term as a misnomer.

There's reasonable practice, there's practice, there's amazingly, fantastic, stupendous practice… But, there's no *best* practice, because who's to say that something that works well in one situation is going to have similar results in another? Who's to say that what is amazing today might not fail completely tomorrow? There are just too many variables.

But this is not a discussion of semantics. It's a discussion of what best practice has come to mean to the HR function; how it is used, and what it is code for.

To illustrate this, let's stay with the example of the Performance Management process, as it's one of the many HR processes that have been modeled on perceived best practice.

Remember when I said it gained momentum in the 1990s? Well, that was largely due to books and keynote addresses by business luminaries such as Jack Welch (GE). In the scramble to add value in new ways, copying proven successful approaches to performance management would surely deliver a quick win?

On paper it sounded great, yet in practice it didn't work out that way.

Let's take a hard look at why.

The first thing we have to understand is that, even though it will claim otherwise, the HR function absolutely *hates* the idea of upsetting people. It's the ultimate *maintain-the-status-quo* function, which can be seen in the risk aversion and bureaucratic overkill of so much of its working practice.

On the surface, we may believe our pursuit of best practice to be about elevation, however the deeper issue is that introducing, or modifying, processes based upon best practices is a game of *"me-too"*, providing a shield behind which HR can hide from its own accountability.

If it was good enough for GE back-in-the-day, the thinking goes, no-one can criticize me for doing it here.

And there's a logic, and undeniable attractiveness, to that argument: *if we didn't design it, we can't be blamed.*

Who's involved... And why?

But there's a deeper pathology at work in HR. And it has to do with the HR value equation, or at least our *perception* of the HR value equation.

Even a cursory look through the articles in our earlier Google search will include a good handful that reference HR as a cost-center rather than profit-center, an administrative overhead running parallel, or even counter, to business objectives.

And you don't have to be a student of the history of HR to know that we don't have a great self-image. Sample HR literature from the last 3 decades and you'll see recurring themes of earning a *"seat at the table"*, proving value, and the unrequited desire to move to a more strategic role.

It's pretty fair to say that, in the majority of organizations, HR as a function suffers from impostor syndrome.

A hard truth to face, but a truth nonetheless.

So, we have a function that seems perpetually obsessed with ensuring/earning/forcing a perception of relevance and credibility…

Now, couple that with rapid technological change in HRIS and B2B services, which is cutting out information brokers across all aspects of society, and you've got a (conscious or sub-conscious) recipe for processes being used as an excuse for continued involvement, and even existence.

Or, in other words, process are deployed to maintain the need to have HR as an organizational gatekeeper.

I really do hope you spent some time in our earlier Google search, because that term will likely have been used, along with form completion, multiple signature approvals, policy guidance, worker handbooks, and all the other markers of gates being well-and-truly kept!

Later in the book, we'll be spending a whole chapter on the question of who does what in a process. Ahead of that though, I want to share a question that I have used throughout my work in HR transformation, both to simplify processes and to challenge deeply-held mindsets:

> ARE YOU INVOLVED BECAUSE YOU'RE JUSTIFIED… OR JUSTIFIED BECAUSE YOU'RE INVOLVED?

Said differently, if any part of your job sounds like *"… because they can't get it done without me…"* then you just might be a bureaucrat!

It's not easy to practice light-touch HR - we are pushing against a heavy weight of functional and organizational pressure to prove relevance, credibility and capability.

A well-designed process reduces unnecessary involvement while simultaneously providing grounded information that, used correctly, can undercut resistance to making change happen.

Now that we've taken a look at some of the internal landmines to delivering high quality process design in HR, let's look at a couple of other insights that have the potential to help you get it done.

A couple of (pretty safe) assumptions

We're going to take a look at change management relating to process design a little later on, but in the early scoping stages of any HR process design initiative, you'll hear quite a bit of resistance due to the perceived risk of upsetting employees, leaders, and other members of HR.

To hear this resistance, you might come to imagine your proposed process design as being akin to defusing a ticking time bomb; that any step forward might cause an inescapable explosion.

I've already mentioned how risk-averse HR is, and this is another example of that in action.

So let me give you a quick antidote in the form of my first assumption:

ASSUMPTION 1: NOBODY CARES ABOUT HR PROCESSES

Frankly, I have yet to meet an employee, people manager or senior leader who is monitoring HR processes just in case anything changes. Similarly rare is the non-HR person who visits the online HRIS portal just for kicks.

Because, nobody cares about HR processes…

Well, that is, nobody cares about HR processes until they try to use one and find that:

    a) It doesn't work

    b) It doesn't make sense

    c) It isn't fair or reasonable

    d) It is way more effort than it should ever take to get something done

Said differently, people only care about HR processes when they're broken or, for our purposes, *poorly designed.*

And, thankfully, we know how to do something about that.

But it is in the doing that we encounter our second safe assumption about HR process design:

ASSUMPTION 2: HR BELIEVES EVERYONE CARES ABOUT HR PROCESSES

We've already talked about it earlier in this chapter, but it is really, really worth reiterating: the main resistance and roadblocks you will meet in designing processes in HR will come from your HR colleagues.

Sometimes it will seem like well-meaning, constructive input, sometimes like unrequested HR leadership course corrections, sometimes like outside-of-the-room passive aggressive mobilization of client business organizations, sometimes like shadow system workarounds, but rarely will it sound like:

"I don't want you to change that process…"

This means that process design initiatives can be something of a minefield for the intrepid explorer.

Now that we know that, though, we can plan to address it - particularly in our input and involvement strategy, and not solely as a line item on our change management plan.

We'll cover all that soon, but before we do, let's take a look at one further area of concern that has to be on radar before we even draw a box on paper.

The system made me do it...

I don't have to tell you that the landscape of HR technology, both in terms of offerings and functionality has gone through a revolution in the last couple of decades. For those who never experienced paper-based HR, it can be hard to even imagine not having an HRIS for employee information and handling, ATS for recruitment, Web Portal for information dissemination, online benefit elections, and on, and on, and on...

And throughout this technological revolution, HR leaders looking to avoid being seen to own the *rocking-of-the-boat* have found an easy scapegoat in the form of new systems.

"We didn't want to do... like this, but the system made us..."

(I'll let you fill in the blanks)

And, actually, it would be great if the system did make change happen, because most of the HRIS out there has been designed and built by people who know what they're doing.

The challenge isn't the system, it's what's done to the system on implementation - most specifically, the area of customization.

You see, HRIS come loaded with a *"vanilla"* process map pre-loaded, one that will fit around 99% of instances if there's not prior art of a similar process running.

Said differently, a start-up HR function that adopted the vanilla processes from a new HRIS would be more likely to be effective and efficient out-of-the-gate than a longer-standing function with clearly established processes.

Why? Workarounds. Customizations. Call-outs. Fudges. Call it what you will, it's where an agreed-upon process has been disagreed with, and the disagreement accepted and respected by officially undermining the process.

HR is notorious for playing *"but what if…"* with processes, another subtle way of resisting change. We're going to talk about that later in the book, in a section I call the *"Blue Sock Clause"*.

For now, though, I'll encourage you to stay aware of when the system is being set up to be blamed, *by the very people who asked for the system to be introduced.*

My bottom line is simple here:

ASSUMPTION 3: TECHNOLOGY IS A SOLUTION/DELIVERY MECHANISM FOR A PROCESS DESIGN BUT IS RARELY, IF EVER, THE DRIVING FORCE

In this chapter, we've taken a quick walk through the landscape of process design in HR. We've taken a look at external opinions of HR, and how process is at the core of most issues. We've identified some cultural pathologies in HR that often compromise, or even derail, process design efforts; these are deeply rooted in risk aversion and blame avoidance. We've also identified a small handful of assumptions that can help provide a solid foundational attitude to process design in HR.

Now, without further ado, let's jump into the methodology itself and how to design effective and efficient HR processes that secure buy-in, commitment and compliance.

PROCESS DESIGN BASICS

What is a process?

A PROCESS IS A CONSISTENT, REPEATABLE SERIES OF STEPS TOWARDS A CLEARLY-DEFINED END-POINT.

Approaches to Process Design

This book is all about an approach to Process Design that works for the vast majority of situations that Human Resources will face; it's tried and fully tested.

Spend any time searching, though, and you will find hundreds, maybe even thousands, of approaches and methodologies for Process Design, each of which have their own unique language and structure. From IT to Manufacturing, from

Education to Business, the solutions range far and wide, and the complexity of methodology doesn't always match the challenge in hand.

As explained earlier, HR is often looking for any reason it can find to NOT have to design the process - and arguing choice of methodology is a very cute avoidance strategy - so we want to adhere to *Keep It Simple* principles here...

DON'T MAKE THINGS MORE COMPLEX
THAN THEY NEED TO BE

Throughout this book, we're going to do just that.

The basic building blocks of Process Design

The first step of keeping it simple is to look at the basic building blocks we'll be using to design our process. At the moment, think of these as categories, which we will flesh out as necessary when we dive deep into examples.

For our purposes, a process will involve one or more of the following factors:

- Information
- Actions
- Decisions
- Roles

Information

For the purposes of the approach laid-out in this book, information represents any data, content and/or message that is generated by, or passed between steps of the process. Information may or may not be captured in online or local data storage systems; including the brains of subject matter experts!

Actions

An action is something that happens, and which typically leads to: a) another action; b) a decision point; or c) a resolution or closure point for the process in question. In any given process, an action may overlap with an action from another process.

Decisions

In our process methodology, we will use decisions specifically to denote a branching point in the process. This may be a go/no-go decision, a yes/no decision, or an if-then decision. While design for software processes allows for iterative decision-making (loops), I've found it easier to ascribe such loops as an action for HR processes; e.g. capturing an Action for *"… thinks about"* and a Decision for *"…makes a decision"*. Such an approach recognizes that we are dealing with human processes here, not machines.

Roles

Given the unhealthy tendency for HR to be self-justifying by being involved in processes, it's really important that we focus on process Roles. Put simply, in process terms, Roles break down who is doing the step, who is involved, who cares about it (and how much). There's a whole section dedicated to this end, but for now, the main thing to know is that we should be as specific as possible in delineating roles, including system touch-points.

The Shape(s) of things to come

Now, if you've ever been close to any formal process design work, you'll have seen shapes and wiring diagrams in the form of a process flow-chart - if you haven't, don't worry, we'll be detailing them over the course of this book.

For now, just know that each of these building blocks can have 1 (or more) graphical representations on a process flow-chart, and in the spirit of keeping things simple, we'll cover each of those when we're talking about real examples; I've no will to help you become a theoretical process designer!

With that said, let's agree a basic definition of what we mean by Process Design.

What is Process Design?

Put simply, Process Design is the sequencing of these building blocks; arranging them in an order that flows from a start-point to an end-point.

This sequencing may be linear (*"do A and then do B"*), or parallel (*"do B while doing C"*):

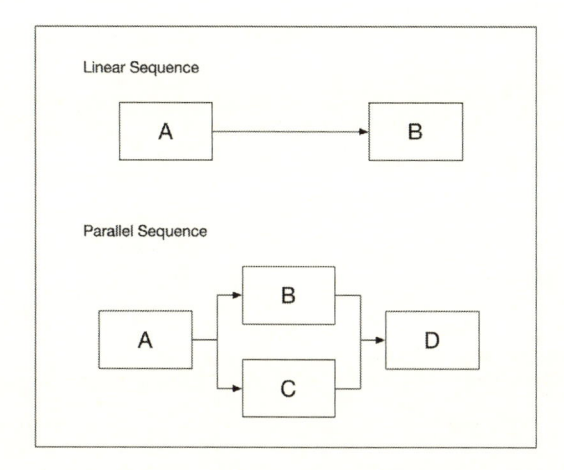

Linear Sequence

A → B

Parallel Sequence

A → B, C → D

Linear sequencing really comes into play when there is an absolute step (i.e. something has to be complete before the next thing can happen - e.g. a Go/No-go decision, such as an authorization.

When designing for efficiency (speed, cost, etc.), parallel sequencing is usually preferable, as things get done at the same time. Be careful of assuming that this is always the case, though - it's really important to make sure there aren't assumed, or hidden dependencies that can force parallel processes into linear flows - we'll talk about this more soon.

For now, it's enough to know that we have blocks that are connected by arrows, and that by following the path we get from the defined start-point to the defined end-point.

LAYING THE GROUNDWORK

Before we get too excited to dive in though, we've much to cover before we put a single building block on a page. Why so? Well, it all comes down to one of my favorite guiding principles; it's as true now as it was when I first started using it over 25 years ago:

WHAT STARTS WELL, ENDS BETTER

Unfortunately, in HR we are often prone to not just running before we can walk, but running before we even know where we want to get to.

Whether it's process design, projects, system implementations or recruitment campaigns, we will often be doing before we know that we started doing.

Why is this? Well, the full answer to that question would take its own book to fully explore, and we already have this book to navigate without heading off down a massive tangent.

So, let's summarize by saying that it's a heady concoction of wanting to add value, feeling under fire, being eager to please, and too busy to do much else than the next thing on the list.

Are there calm waters of applied strategic HR out there, where every action and decision occupies its own reasonable space and time? Where every offered *"seat-at-the-table"* is filled *con mucho gusto?*

Maybe but, speaking frankly, I've yet to find one.

Sure, I've met people - sometimes delusional people - who want to tell me they're living that particular dream, but scratch the surface and… Well, color me skeptical.

Which is why *"what starts well, ends better"* is so powerful for HR.

When we focus on starting well, we take the time - even if only a slight pause - to give ourselves a direction, target and goal which, in turn, informs our plan of action, expectations and accountabilities.

Starting well lays the groundwork for decisions, resource calls and, perhaps most importantly, stakeholder management; the place where so many HR initiatives turn up DOA.

And the primary, most important aspect of *"what starts well, ends better"* is a single word: *WHY?*

For the sake of what (and who)?

It's Monday morning, and the HR group lifts its collective head from the email inbox to take stock of what else is on the agenda. Someone mentions calmly that a process might possibly benefit from some refinement.

All right, we know that's not how these things come to light.

It's much more likely that an angry voicemail, email or text has dropped like a bomb and, depending upon the organizational level of the person making the complaint, everyone's gone into crisis mode to fix what's broken.

After a flurry of discussion and sidelong glances, things are left with the current process owner to manage, while everyone else moves on to the next fire burning in the inbox.

Sound familiar? For most people in HR this is a fairly regular experience because:

PROCESS DESIGN/REDESIGN IS OFTEN A RESPONSE TO A PAIN POINT

This is really important to understand.

In everyday life, not the halcyon sales pitch of HR Transformation initiatives, HR processes are shaped and flexed because someone somewhere isn't happy about how HR is getting something done.

Which means we don't often ask the most important question we should:

WHY ARE WE DOING THIS PROCESS?

We could dive deep into the waters of HR history here, discussing the roots of the function in general personnel management and employee relations, how responses to increasing workplace regulation were enshrined in policy and procedure, compliance-based training and paper-based administration.

We could talk of how management were, for decades, quite happy to off-lay anything that remotely touched people, teams or organizations to the HR function, who weren't given voice or chance to suggest otherwise.

We could go there, but we don't need to, because we all know that history, and it's wide and deep legacy on our self-image and the opinions of others; after all, we did do our Google search earlier on!

Let's summarize by saying that the prevalent knee-jerk response in HR is:

I'VE BEEN ASKED, SO I MUST DO

Said differently, it's *"Fire… Ready… Aim…"*

If we are to break this decades-old behavioral and organizational norm, we have to stop reacting so much. We have to learn to assert our value.

And value begins with asking:

WHY ARE WE DOING THIS PROCESS?

Reasonable responses to this question might include:

- The process fulfills a legal requirement
- The process enables front-line managers to manage
- The process protects us from potential risks
- The process delivers upon our colleague value proposition
- The process improves individual, team, and/or organizational performance
- The process supports the terms and conditions of employment

And, of course, any single process might contribute under a number of these headings.

Take a read of the list again, though, and see if you can see what's missing…

When we ask *"why are we doing this process?"*, the wrong answer, the unjustified answer, the unreasonable answer is:

BECAUSE WE'VE ALWAYS DONE IT

You've no idea how easy that was to write. And yet, take any process that HR currently delivers, and ask the question… What you'll hear, no matter how justified and passionate the response, will be some version of *"because we've always done it."*

For example, why is HR involved in the recruitment process?

Take some time on that question alone and see if you don't come up against something that sounds like a sacred cow - i.e. *"But HR always does recruitment…"*

Note, I'm not arguing one way or the other, I'm just using this as an example of how we just don't ask the right question at the outset.

And even if we do, go one step further and ask *"why are we doing this process like that?"* and you'll immediately hear something along the lines of *"because that's how we've always done it…"*

Unfortunately, we've bumped into the stubborn *status quo* of day-to-day HR, where boats remain resolutely un-rocked until the complaints and pain points become too much to bear.

Yet, at the same time, we coach leaders who seek continuous improvement, we learn all we can about six-sigma and AGILE project management, we talk a good game of agility and flexibility.

And our processes grind on. And on.

So, let's go back to our long-list of *"whys"* to see how we can begin to break the deadlock of the *status quo*.

Fundamentally, these boil down to 3 core areas of focus:

WHY ARE WE DOING THIS PROCESS?

- Individual, Team, and/or Organizational Capability
- Employment support and Colleague Value Proposition
- Legal requirement/compliance/protection

An initial glance at these may feel reductive; is it really that simple?

Well, let's flip things on their head and turn these into questions:

- How does this process enable individual, team or organizational capability?
- How does this process support employment and the colleague value proposition?
- How does this process protect us from risks, including legal compliance?

Do these questions begin to sound like guiding principles to process design? They really should, and when we choose to start well, we ask these questions first, because they'll not only inform our destination but also the shape and style of our process.

For example, a process designed for legal compliance may include multiple authorization points, signatures and checkboxes (think of your average tax form), whereas a process that enables managers to manage situations based upon circumstances and completely within their own accountability/discretion, may have a much lighter-touch, with very few check-points or absolute decisions.

In redesign, we might use these questions to unpick a legacy process. For example, benefits enrollment. What may have been a lengthy legal-compliance style hangover from paper-based forms can now be considered from the vantage point of how it supports the colleague value proposition. And the process may be redesigned to feel much more like an online purchasing flow (think virtual concierge).

And, of course, there are situations where a process will be some combination of the three areas.

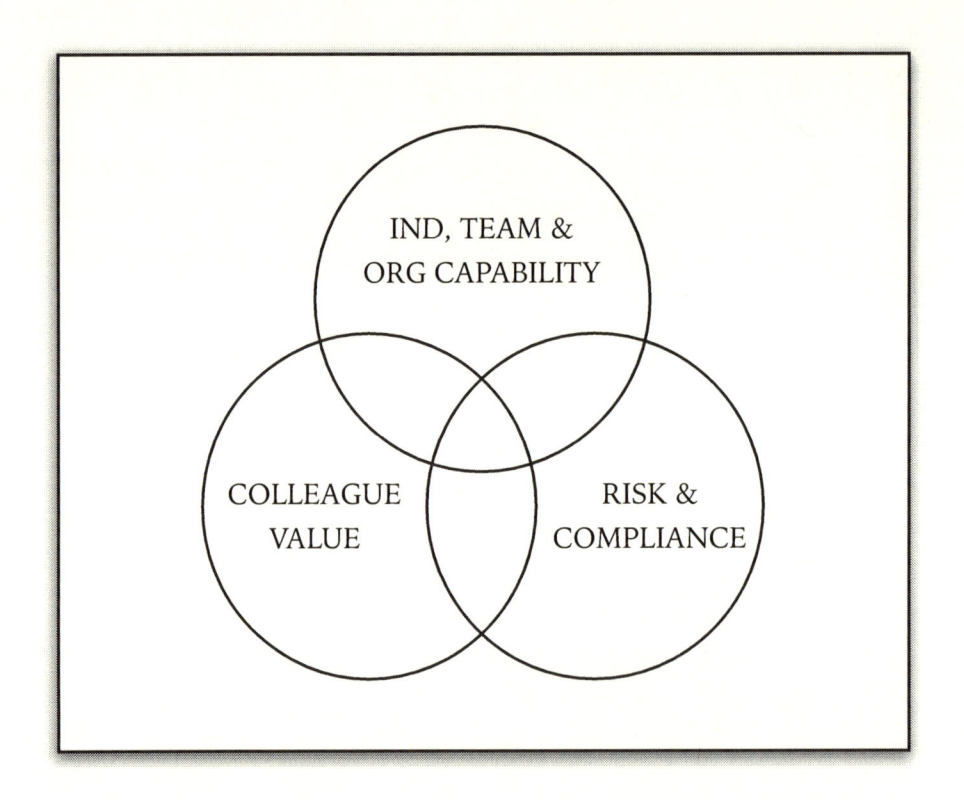

```
        IND, TEAM &
        ORG CAPABILITY


  COLLEAGUE              RISK &
    VALUE             COMPLIANCE
```

For example, we may focus upon a team-led working culture that proves attractive to colleagues compared to other companies. A process for localized team reward and recognition would obviously bridge both Capability and Value spheres. In fact, there may be an added flavor to such a process in terms of monitoring fairness and just treatment - an example of risk mitigation and compliance.

This quick example shows how important it is to keep sight of these guiding principles - the *"whys"* of our process - at all stages of any process design initiative.

Who's yelling loudest?

And so things begin to get real... I wasn't joking earlier when I shared that most process design comes about because of pain points. And, if you've spent any time in HR, at any level, you'll have experienced the HR Business Partner who walks into a meeting, or even just into the office, with a slightly panicked look on their face saying something along the lines of:

> "<INSERT SENIOR LEADER NAME> JUST TRIED TO <INSERT PROCESS NAME>, AND THEY'RE NOT HAPPY…"

I've seen it too many times to count. Have you? Maybe not. But let me ask, have you ever heard complaints about:

- The speed of the recruitment process
- The lack of data to support HR decision making
- Benefit elections gone wrong
- Payroll being late
- Performance Management cycles being convoluted and overwhelming
- Promotions taking way to many authorization steps
- Lack of flexibility for managers who want to differentially reward performance

And yes, the list could go on. And on.

But we're not here to join the chorus of disapproval of HR process effectiveness and efficiency, we're here to do something about it.

So, instead of lamenting the current state, let's pick apart what's actually happening here.

It's all about a couple of troublesome biases that underpin focus in HR.

The first bias is *immediacy*.

Put simply, most members of HR are running in real-time, swamped by inbox overload, and unable to get everything done. The net result is a lived reality of *"whatever's next…"* and both clients and HR have reached acceptance of this as the uncomfortable norm.

And, in this norm, both clients and HR have learned to play the game of *"who shouts loudest is more likely to receive a response."*

Immediacy adds an extra boost to this game: *"who is shouting loudest right now?"*

In a limited bandwidth situation, the loudest voice I'm hearing right now is the one to whom I'll respond.

Ready to juice the game even further?

Let's add in a bias for *seniority*.

If John from Manufacturing complains about the payroll process, we may handle the complaint and move on. We may even dismiss the complaint because we know that *"the process will figure it out at some point."*

Or, we may play the toxic HR game of *"lay the blame"*.

Either way, John's complaint won't climb very high up our flag-pole.

But what if the complaint comes from Cindy, our Chief Finance Officer?

Will we dismiss Cindy as just having to wait. Will we shrug our shoulders and tell her: *"I don't know, you'll have to speak to Payroll…"*

Of course we won't. Because HR is too far in thrall to seniority; we simply do not respond to all levels of the organization the same way. We may want to believe we do… but we really don't.

In terms of process, what this means is that when John complains, he'll just have to suck it up and wait for things to get sorted out. When Cindy complains, however, the process must be broken so badly that it requires immediate surgery.

Now, when we combine *Immediacy* and *Seniority* we get a very heady stew indeed!

Said differently, when Cindy's shouting down the phone - or writing a very terse email - demanding that her HR Business Partner do something (anything!) to make this thing work, you just know that the process, and the process owner, are in the gunsights.

And there may well be an immediate fix that will stop the bleeding. But the landscape is littered with processes that have been patched up and customized just to get through the latest hiccup, difficulty or complaint.

Listen carefully though; while they may help the short-term pain:

BAND-AIDS ARE NOT A LONG-TERM FIX

So, in the daily firefight, triage and treat as necessary, but don't lose sight of the long-term - and that means healthy, fit-for-purpose processes.

Fit-for-purpose processes

Let's pick a process, it doesn't really matter which one... Got one? Good, let me ask some questions.

When was it created? When was it last reviewed? When was it last designed from the ground-up? When was it tested against the value of its outcomes? How is the value of its outcomes measured? How is the efficiency of the process measured?

Can you answer those questions easily? Immediately?

I don't expect so, and you wouldn't be alone. You see, the majority of processes in HR are defined at a point in time and then frozen in place until one of two things happen: 1) they break catastrophically; or 2) something external to the process forces a change.

Sure, annual processes like performance management, or the compensation cycle, might get a light dust-off every year, but that's more likely to be about updating the milestones such as submission deadlines, etc. than it is to be about designing the process.

Now, I'm not about to go on a rant about continuous improvement in HR - and you won't find me pushing for Kaizen, DMAIC, Six Sigma, or any other structured methodology for informed improvement.

I'd like to believe that HR processes were ready for such approaches, but in my experience we are so far from having a) structure to our process delivery; and b) measurable process factors such as throughput, turnaround, etc. that any data-driven improvement is, at best, wishful thinking.

So, if we accept that a rigorous structured approach to process efficiency and effectiveness is beyond our immediate scope, we have to fall back to a simple question: *is this process fit-for-purpose?*

Believe it or not, according to the various online sources, the term *"fit-for-purpose"* only began to appear widely during the 2000s, though it feels like it's been around much longer. Certainly, in my experience, it's not the norm to apply the term to HR processes. So let's take a look at a common definition:

FIT-FOR-PURPOSE (ADJ.): APPROPRIATE, AND OF A NECESSARY STANDARD, FOR ITS INTENDED USE

Hopefully, given everything we've talked about so far, it should be immediately apparent why this is a GREAT frame within which to consider HR processes.

Appropriateness

Let's look at a quick example.

As we've discussed, in the old days, everything people- and employment- related was administrated through HR; Sick days, Vacation, Jury Duty, and on, and on… We may think of these as data fields in our HRIS now but, not so long ago, these were form-based approval chains (with carbon copy paper included!)

Given what we now know about managerial empowerment, is it appropriate for HR to be involved in the approval of a Vacation Day for an employee?

Depending on your organization size and internal accountabilities, you may be answering that with a resounding *"yes!"* Or, you may be saying that that's the very last thing that HR should be involved in…

Either way, the point is not an absolute *"either/or"*, it's about knowing whether the process is appropriate or not. In other words, appropriateness swings back to what we discussed earlier: *are you involved because you're justified, or justified because you're involved?*

While this may be a simple example, I hope you can see that this is a quick and incisive test of HR processes. Later in the book, we'll be talking about how to organize process design efforts, so for now I'll just say that any strategic HR planning off-site, or process design kick-off meeting, should include some time spent to assessing and discussing the appropriateness of existing processes.

Necessary Standard

I love the fact that this is called out in our definition of *"fit-for-purpose"*, because it could have been left under the umbrella of *Appropriateness*.

Let's get playful with our simple example of Vacation approval in order to illustrate the point - after all, who said we couldn't have a little fun?

We've already decided that HR doesn't need to be directly involved in the approval, because that wouldn't be appropriate. But what happens once the Vacation has been approved? Well, in our scenario, let's agree that fact needs to be tracked in our HRIS. How does the data get there?

In version one of our process, the Manager visits his team dashboard and enters the approved dates and times of the Vacation.

In version two of our process, the Manager visits his team dashboard and clicks the *"I wish to approve Vacation days for an employee"* link.

Immediately, in the HR suite, a bell rings, and a red light starts flashing.

After a quick huddle, the HR Business Partner for the Manager's department, Malcolm, heads for the door, pausing only to put on some running shoes and grab a fur lined cushion.

A quick sprint later and Malcolm arrives at the Manager's office, slightly out of breath. He kneels and offers the cushion to the Manager, who proceeds to place a completed and signed Vacation Approval Form on said cushion. Malcolm stands and walks backwards out of the office, bowing all the way.

A second sprint, and the magical form arrives back at the HR suite, where it is passed to an HR data specialist for encoding into the HRIS, enshrined for all time as a statement of record.

Both versions accomplish the same thing, but our absurd second version is definitely overkill compared to version one! Said differently, version two is of a completely *UNnecessary* standard for the task in hand.

The flip side to overkill is when a process is underdone, where there isn't enough care and attention to the task in hand. A good example of this would be a disciplinary process that was so loose that it didn't provide sufficient support for subsequent legal defense, or a promotion process that does not include specific reference to guidelines to ensure fairness of treatment.

A simple way to think of an underdone process is that it provides multiple opportunities for unexpected variance, unexpected outcomes, or even opportunities for breakdowns.

A process is of a necessary standard when it is just enough - neither overkill nor underdone - to deliver as expected.

In fact, we can pull from the Project Management lexicon here and say that a process is of a necessary standard when it:

- Delivers TIMEly outcomes
- Ensures QUALITY of outcomes
- Minimizes COST of outcomes

Going back to our assessment, this provides three simple questions to ask of any existing process:

- Is it fast enough?
- Does it have the right checks and balances?
- Does it require the minimal resource necessary for completion?

An absolute yes to all three? Then your process is very likely of the necessary standard!

If, however, your process doesn't pass this sniff test then it's not of the necessary standard and, by definition, it's not fit-for-purpose. And if you happen to also find it's not appropriate, then the route forward is clear: *process design*.

A Strong Foundation

So, if our aim is a fit-for-purpose process, what can we do to give ourselves the best chances of success?

We've covered a lot of ground about the *"why"* of process design in this chapter and, as we're not yet beginning to turn our sights to the *"what"* and *"how"*, I would suggest there are two key take-aways.

Don't short-change process design

There's no easy way to say this. We are where we are because processes are not fit-for-purpose. They either weren't designed well in the first place, or began to break somewhere down the line.

From experience, the root cause of the issue was that we evolved from a place/time when the act of getting things done wasn't designed at all and so, at some point during organizational growth, a process was described to force fit over existing behaviors and roles. When that happened, it very much was NOT process design!

So, if the common definition of insanity is doing the same thing over again and expecting different results, let's agree not to do that when it comes to your next process design.

Make it real! Design the heck out of that process!

And that means two things: *giving yourself space*, and *giving yourself time*.

Whatever it takes - depending on scale and scope, it could be putting time on the calendar, forming a team, right through to announcing a full-blooded process re-engineering initiative - be sure to do it.

By creating the space (either physically or metaphorically), you enable the process design to be completed fully - i.e. arrive at a fit-for-purpose process.

By creating the space, you identify who is doing the work of process design, removing tinkering thumbs from the pie at the same time.

By creating the space, you prevent the waves of concerned stakeholders (most of whom are in HR, remember) who would have you customize the process before its even designed.

Alongside space, we have to give time for process design.

We largely ended up where we are because of *"too busy"* and *"just get it done"*. So again, let's not do that.

In HR particularly, process design can come under time crunch from a number of directions. The first is the nature of everyone running just to stand still. It's hard to carve out time in the short-term for gains in the medium- to long-term. It just is.

But a second aspect of time crunch rears its head when we start the work of process design - and it lies in a complex area of personal and professional identity, and ingrained expectations.

You see, HR is the ultimate just-in-time, right-where-you-are function - most of the time, we're dealing with what's right in front of us; the rubber that is already hitting the road.

So when we move to an abstract, virtual exercise such as process design it can feel a little bit like spinning off into space. By its very nature, process design is all about imagining the doing, rather than doing.

And it can be very uncomfortable for those who have been used to *Fire… Ready… Aim* to spend a lot of time asking *"What would Aim look like?"*

Later in the book, I'm going to share my thoughts on how to best involve people in a process design initiative - it's really important, and deserves its very own section - for now, though, let me summarize by saying that I've sat in many, many rooms watching members of HR get very, very twitchy as we reorganize boxes on a flow diagram and debate each change, before locking down a decision.

This is not overkill, it's how processes get designed. And it feels very different to the day-to-day adrenaline rush of *"what's next?"*

So, it's really important to a) make sure whoever is doing the design work has the requisite skills and behavioral fortitude to do the work; and b) knows they have the time to do the work right.

By creating the time, you reinforce your expectation of a fit-for-purpose process.

By creating the time, you protect against future-state band-aids.

By creating the time, you increase the likelihood of right-first-time, and lay a path of continuous improvement that will take much LESS time in the future.

The critical importance of sponsorship

The second key takeaway of this chapter is that of sponsorship, and how critical it is to getting *anything* done in HR.

Why so? Well, simply put, because the prevailing tides within HR and external pressures upon HR are, more often than not, focused upon maintaining the status quo, no matter how painful it may be, someone somewhere has to commit to: *"this is going to happen"*.

And that someone has to have both organizational (position) and political (relationship) power to back up that commitment, or the effort will ultimately come to nothing, and change will not happen.

As an aside, I have definitely seen many, and been involved in a few, process design projects that have ultimately failed the sponsorship test; this particular battle-scar is hard earned.

This is why I can't stress this enough:

WANT TO CHANGE A PROCESS? GET A SPONSOR

So, what does a sponsor do exactly?

A sponsor provides an *"umbrella"* within which the work necessary to deliver agreed objectives can be completed successfully. A sponsor authorizes the work, represents the work, and shields the work sufficiently to enable success.

For our purpose, the Process Sponsor is the person who formally states *"a fit-for-purpose process will be designed…"* and who subsequently creates the space and the time for that to happen.

The Process Sponsor may, or may not, be directly involved in the design work itself. And, at any time, they may be called upon to resolve escalated issues, provide vision, guidance and reassurance to process design team members, and even make executive decisions relating to risks affecting, or arising from, the process design.

Put bluntly, when it comes to any specific process design, the buck stops with the Sponsor.

In *"Project Management For Human Resources: The Structure and Art of getting things done in HR"*, I provide significant detail on how to select and involve Stakeholders in a project, and I won't retread that ground here - though I will say that the larger, more impactful the process you're designing, the more you will want to wrap your process design activities in a formal project management framework, particularly when it comes to engaging stakeholders both along the way, and when implementing process changes.

The role of the Sponsor in Process Design

Let's look at Sponsorship specific to process design, and some key inflection points. To do so, we'll use a process flow!

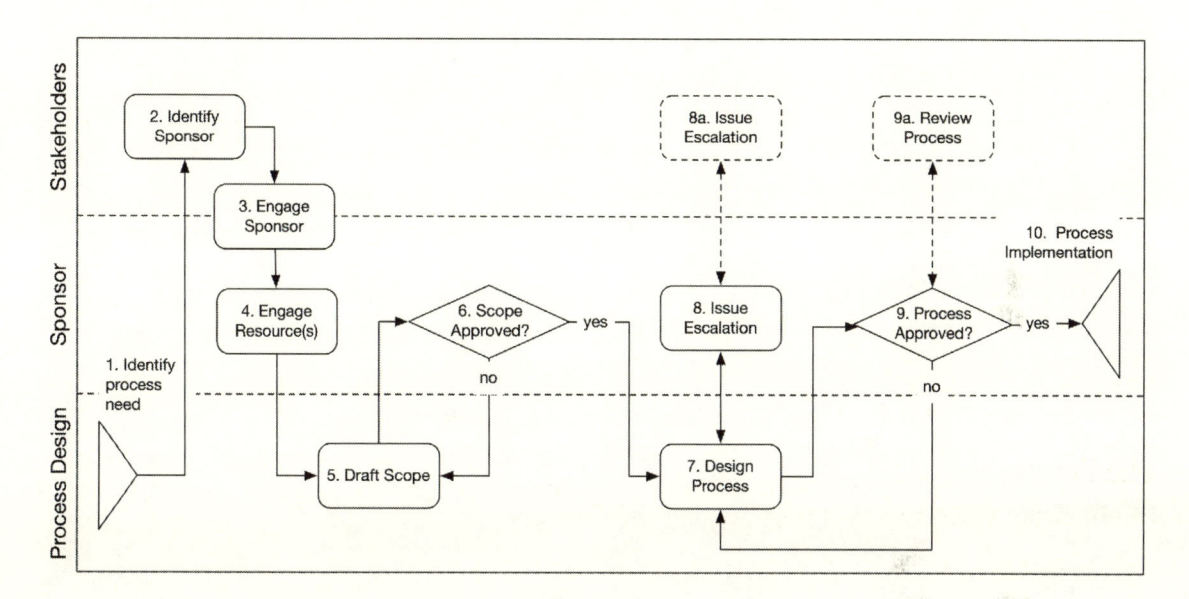

I've deliberately kept this simple, so as to focus on the role of the Sponsor, but suffice to say that, while each process design effort will have it's own nuances, the overall flow will be very similar to what is represented here. Let's walk through it step by step.

The first thing to note is the swim-lane construct of roles in this meta-process. We'll be discussing the use of swim-lanes in process mapping a little later in the book; for now, it's enough to know that each horizontal lane represents the activities and/or decisions pertaining to a specific role.

At the bottom, *Process Design*, we are not talking about an individual who designs the process, but instead a bucket of roles and activity that might interact with the Sponsor.

At the top, *Stakeholders*, is a bucket to include business and HR stakeholders, one of whom may ultimately become the Sponsor for the resulting process design initiative.

The only singular role identified here is that of Sponsor itself, which we'll discuss further as we break-down this process.

1. **Identify process need**

The need for a process to be designed can come from anywhere. It could be employee feedback, it could be data-driven insights, it could be legal regulation, and on, and on…

Whatever the source, the important point to note here is that this is a trigger for the process of process design, and nothing more. Said differently, nothing has or is happening yet!

2. **Identify Sponsor**

So, thanks to step 1, we are newly aware of a process needing to be designed, and the first step is for the appropriate stakeholders to answer the question: *"who is on the hook for making sure this gets done?"*

Quite often, particularly where there is some structural organization such as Centers of Expertise (COE), or functional specialities, the Sponsor may be easy to identify. For example, a change to the external recruitment process would typically be sponsored by the Talent Acquisition lead.

Sometimes, though, the lines are blurred. For example, take a look at the internal recruitment/transfers process - isn't that also under Talent Acquisition, after all they post the jobs and manage both the external and internal pipelines? Well, yes... But what if there's a Talent Planning and Succession COE that wants to purposefully move people internally? Who sponsors the process then?

The answer is that the Stakeholder(s) involved - usually, but not always, the HR leadership team - need to make the call on where the buck stops.

Be careful here because, as we discussed earlier, HR has a tendency to avoid tough conversations by just involving people, and in process design having multiple people with authority to call the shots on critical decisions is a recipe for a compromised, inefficient process.

As you can probably tell, I'm of the strong opinion that Sponsorship should be singular - i.e. a Sponsor, not Sponsors.

If the process stakeholders do decide on joint Sponsors, agree up-front how you plan to resolve tie-breaks - where one decides one direction, the other another - including *"veto power"*. If the answer here is that, when that happens, we'll go and ask someone else (e.g. the CHRO), then you're not really speaking to the right Sponsor for the initiative!

As an aside, you might be surprised how many times I've been in HR process design discussions and ended up playing an *"escalation game"* that ultimately would have the CEO involved in making contentious process designs decisions. Take such discussions and debates for what they are: avoidance of accountability.

Said differently, sponsorship should be local to the process and accountable for changes.

There is one situation where identifying a Sponsor can be particularly thorny.

There may come a time - particularly in HR Transformation initiatives - where the *project* Sponsor's authority supersedes that of the current process owner. This happens because the need for transformation is forcing change into the *status quo*, which is often resident in turf wars and power plays relating to processes.

When this is the case, there can be a knee-jerk impulse to invite the process owner to be a joint sponsor for the specific design. This happens from some combination of not wanting to hurt feelings, while also keeping *"enemies"* where they can be seen.

When this happens, there's an early warning sign for which I'd encourage you to monitor.

It'll feel something like this. In all joint discussions, the process owner and HR leadership will seem in *"violent agreement"* that a process needs to be overhauled. However, away from those discussions, the process owner will tell you that *"not that much needs to change, really."*

As you go through the process design phase, you'll continually be told that current steps are necessary, and must be performed in the existing order and functionality.

Put simply, though publicly agreeing to process redesign, privately the process owner is a primary resistor.

Why is this the case? Well it all boils down to the reality of achieving transformational change in HR - where everyone talks about wanting it to happen, while simultaneously avoiding/resisting the necessary actions and decisions to make it happen.

As a process designer, you do not want to end up answering to two masters, one of whom may be seeking to maintain their place and position power, while the other may be seeking to radically reshape the function.

Before taking any action, then, agree where the buck stops and make sure all involved understand that's the case.

Bottom line: I can't stress enough how important it is to identify and agree the singular sponsor for any initiative, especially as the scale and scope of the initiative expand.

3. Engage Sponsor

There, see how easy it was to identify a Sponsor? Well, now it's time to let them know they've been identified, and tell them what's expected (which is summarized in the process flow above).

Who does that?

Well, there's no hard and fast rule, but given our rule of thumb on where the buck stops, the simplest way to think about who engages the Sponsor is who will be on the hook if the Sponsor fails. Typically, this will be the person who actually manages the Sponsor.

For example, if the process concerns relocation benefits, then the Benefits COE lead may be identified as the Sponsor (with a member of their team set to design the process). If the Benefits COE reports into the VP of Total Reward, then that's who will engage the Sponsor to set expectations.

Note that I use the above as an example, and your answer to *"who does that?"* may well be different, but it should follow your organizational norms around goal-setting and accountability; this has to be a real expectation, not loose and fluffy.

Once again, in wider HR Transformation efforts, the Sponsor may be being deployed as a wider change agent, in which case, the CHRO or even senior business executive leaders may want to deliver the critical messages.

Whatever is appropriate to the situation, organization and individuals involved, this step is all about making expectations and consequences crystal clear.

4. Engage Resource(s)

Now that the Sponsor has been identified, and has no doubt as to what they're expected to achieve, it's time to actually talk to people who will, or at least may, get the work done.

I'm a fan of keeping things small and focused until they need to be larger and wide-screen. For this reason, if the sense is that there will be a need for a process design team - for example, if multiple transactional processes are to be designed at once - then, at this stage, I would engage only the proposed Process Design lead, leaving the team size and membership to be considered in step 5, the drafting of scope.

So, with that said, who should serve as your Process Design lead? There isn't a simple answer to this, because of the context we've already discussed. For speed of design, it should be pretty obvious that it's always better to try and use process-local knowledge and expertise. However, for the same reason we might choose to use a Sponsor external to the organizational ownership of the process, we might choose to use a Process Design lead with a similar aim: a *"fresh set of eyes"*.

For me, it's easier to assemble a long-list of potential leads, and then use a simple set of questions to begin to narrow-down the field:

- Who has the skills to lead process design activity?
- To what extent does the process need significant overhaul; who has the innovative edge to push the envelope?
- To what extent might the current process owners/hierarchy impede process design; who has the organizational credibility to influence, and agility to navigate through that particular minefield?

- To what extent might the process redesign offer a learning/developmental experience to those not well-versed in the process subject matter; from our talent/succession planning, who might best benefit from going deep?

Once the process design lead is identified, it's up to the Sponsor to both engage them around expectations for the process design initiative; AND engage their management hierarchy to clear space, time and expectations for the process design work.

This latter point is really important because, if skipped, it can lead to significant issues down the road. It's very rare that a process design lead will be seconded full-time to the process design effort - it happens, but typically, that'll look more like a secondment to an enterprise-wide initiative, with potential back-fill to the sending organization.

If the process design lead does end up designing the process in addition to the *"day job"*, you can bet that, as soon as the pressure goes up in the day job, the importance of the process design will be de-prioritized. At this stage, the lead will either extend their working hours, at risk of burn-out, or just plain not get the process done.

Either way it's a loss.

It's essential then, that the manager of the process design lead helps set and reinforce expectations of commitment to the process design work, including how to carve out the time and focus to deliver - this may require redistribution of work among a team or, potentially, some element of back-fill.

5. Draft Scope

So, we know who's on the strategic hook, and we know who's on the tactical hook. It's about time to have them understand just what they've signed up for!

An alternative view is that this is the point where both Sponsor and Process Design Lead formally take ownership of the project and shape it to their intent.

This is an interactive, iterative step where the initial need that triggers the process of process design is stripped back to it's bare bones - we're going to talk about the how of this step in the next chapter, as our focus here is on the Sponsor.

The main thing to know is that, although the Sponsor may be involved in scoping discussions, the work should mainly fall on the shoulders of the process design lead.

6. Scope Approved ? (Y/N)

This step occurs in an iterative cycle with the previous step. At some point, the Sponsor will make a decision that the scope is good to go, and that the next step can start.

Depending on the scale and scope of the process, this step may include a round of review and endorsement from key stakeholders, however I've not indicated that on the process map because I didn't want to infer that it should always happen. The Sponsor will have to be a judge of how important it is to share scope at this point - and in some transformational initiatives, scope should absolutely not be shared, because of the risk of starting up the rumor-mill.

If the early steps of the Sponsorship process we're considering are done well, the Sponsor should be empowered to make the scope go/no-go decision on behalf of the organization.

7. Design Process

When it comes to the actual design of the process, the Sponsor should rarely, if ever be involved directly. Their role is to champion the process design and not to do it!

Does this mean they are not in the loop on what's happening? Absolutely not - in fact it's critical that they are up-to-speed on current design status, issues, risks and decisions.

They're just not doing the design work.

8. Issue Escalation

That said, there is one place the Sponsor must be ready to act: *Issue Escalation*.

Simply defined, an issue is something that is happening, and that impacts the process design team's ability to move forward[i].

In most process design work there are three main issues that will arise:

- Shortfall of resources
- Inability to access information
- Issues relating to particular process steps

The first issue is a purely managerial challenge, and the Sponsor may be called upon to help expedite the log-jam, either by working with other leaders to ensure commitments are delivered or by finding alternative means of delivery.

---

[i] I cover Issue & Risk Management at length in "Project Management For Human Resources - the STRUCTURE and ART of getting things done in HR"

Our earlier example of a process design lead being caught out when the *"day job"* gets busy would fall under this family of issues.

When it comes to access to information, the issue could be two-fold. In the first situation, the information may not exist, or may not be readily available. HR is notoriously bad at deriving and driving processes based upon data, so quite often project teams are left designing in a black-box, because few data-led insights are available.

As an aside, this is one of the reasons why structured process improvement approaches such as Six-Sigma find it hard to gain traction in HR - it's not the fault of the method, but more so that the raw substrate isn't available.

When information doesn't exist, there's not really much the Sponsor can do, except be aware and supportive of recommendations from the process design team that aim to address the issue.

Where the Sponsor can play a powerful role, however, is in those situations where the information does exist, but is not available because there is a gate-keeper holding back the team. This should be expected in transformational initiatives, but it can also show up in smaller-scale process designs.

This happens when there's a specialist or leader in place who views the process as their own, and who therefore doesn't respect the formal authority vested in the process design team - we'll talk later about how to neatly prepare for and address this before it even becomes a problem.

When such an issue is escalated to the Sponsor though, it's important to focus on why - i.e. that the project team need the information. Period. Although getting that information may put the cat among the pigeons of HR leadership and the wider function, that's not the project's issue or fault. So, the Sponsor has to play their umbrella role here, protecting the project from unwelcome attack.

The final area of issue resolution comes in the form of implications of process steps.

For example, the process design team may identify that a new IT solution has potential to help a process step move faster, at better quality, or reduced overall cost. However, in this scenario, they may not know whether system implementation is within scope.

By escalating this issue to the Sponsor, they are calling for an interim guiding decision on whether to consider that in the design or not. Depending on the step itself, this may be a critical steer for the team - i.e. the process looks completely different given the answer - hence Sponsor (and potentially Stakeholder) involvement.

Earlier we talked about whether internal transfer of talent might fall under Talent Acquisition or Talent Planning - this would be another example of how this last group of issues arise: *organizational implications*.

While I raise this here, we're going to dive a little deeper into this subject in later in the book and, because it underpins a significant pathological behavior in HR process design initiatives, you'll find that it fully deserves its own section!

9. Process Approved? (Y/N)

In a similar way to scope definition, the process is iteratively presented and discussed with the Sponsor until ready for approval. We're going to take time to describe just what that means in the next few chapters.

The main thing to know here is that the Sponsor approves the process. Period.

They may, or may not, involve other stakeholders in the decision, and there may, or may not, be wider communication, but the buck stops with the Sponsor - which is why we were so careful in selecting the right person up front!

10. Process Implementation

The final role of the Sponsor is to support implementation of the process. Quite often, this will be in a figurehead role - through formal and informal communications - but it may also fall into helping with specific change management activity such as dealing with key stakeholders.

And, though not mentioned as a separate step in our process flow, the Sponsor is accountable for ensuring the process design team knows that they're done, providing feedback directly to team members and their managerial chains, as well as ensuring process maintenance plans and resources are implemented (something we'll talk about a little later in the book).

Managing the (sometimes hostile) landscape

So, we've committed to making time for process design, and we've ensured the level of sponsorship that we know we'll need along the way; we're ready to go, right?

Not quite. It's true that, by putting those things in place, we've dramatically increased our potential for long-term success, but we have to acknowledge the reality of the HR landscape.

You see, thanks to the risk aversion and blame avoidance we discussed earlier in the book, you may well find that there are individuals, teams, groups, or even the very leaders who asked you to fix the process, who prove more than a little resistant to the process design work.

This resistance shows up in subtle ways, and can be cloaked in seemingly helpful offers and advice.

But don't be mistaken, it is resistance.

To paraphrase Peter Block (*"Flawless Consulting"*, 1981)…

RESISTANCE IS AN EMOTION THAT HAS FOUND NO MEANS OF EXPRESSION

Said differently, the resistance is typically a reflection of an unexpressed fear, and you can find yourself firefighting symptoms of the resistance (the FIGHT or FLIGHT) and miss the root cause (what's scary and why).

Remember, resistance tries to slow things down, or even bring them to a complete halt (got to maintain the *status quo*!) and, as we take a look at some of the ways such resistance shows up in HR process design, think of it as your early warning system.

While resistance can be nuanced in how it shows up, when it comes to process design, I think of these as the main food groups:

- Questioning the method
- Changing what's changing
- Boiling the ocean
- Defending the current state
- Over involvement
- Designing to protect

And, for sure, like a good Venn diagram, all of these can find some level of overlap. Still, by considering each in isolation, we can hope to spot the tell-tale indicators of which resistance play is in action. Let's look at each of our main food groups in some detail.

Questioning the method

The first flag you may experience is a seemingly overwhelming desire to understand just how you're going to go about designing the process. What method, from which school of process design, involving who, for how long, and on, and on…

The game here is to ask questions because, if I'm asking questions, we're not designing processes.

You should know that just now, I did an online search for *"process design methodologies"* and got around 78.5 million hits in 0.6 seconds. That's a LOT of potential questions about your method!

My antidote for this resistance is to be very clear about the method we're using, and that I'm always open to learning anything that may improve the method. I actually bake such learning into my project meetings (an approach I cover in detail in *"Project Management For Human Resources"*).

That said, I'm also very blunt about calling this resistance by simply stating that we'll learn as we go, not before we head out. Remember, at this stage, we have Sponsorship and we've agreed scope, so we have organizational authority to get going.

Sometimes, you have to choose to be a steam-roller.

Changing what's changing

This is an interesting one, particularly when the impact of the process is wide-ranging, there are multiple people on the team, and involvement of Subject Matter Experts.

What it looks like is assessing the appropriateness of any step based not on how it contributes to the process, but on how difficult it will be to get people to do it, or how painful it will be to get them to change their behavior.

So, instead of designing the process well, we see a push to compromise the process up front. As an aside, historically, this is how so many HR processes end up Dead-On-Arrival out of the gate.

One major red flag for this is happening is when people on the design team, or subject matter experts, insert human touch-points that aren't necessary (e.g. an HR Business Partner reviewing job offer paperwork before a recruiter sends it to the candidate). In essence this is placing a *"comfort blanket"* in the process to, theoretically, soften the blow of the next step.

In essence, when this behavior shows up, it's actually revisiting the scope of the process design. Another reason for strong Sponsorship and authorization of process design.

As I mentioned, *Change What's Changing* shows up tooth-and-claw when we are designing a process that delivers a painful outcome.

For example, imagine we are designing a process for re-selection of existing employees during a reduction-in-force (RIF).

At its core, this is actually fairly simple - identify what jobs will exist after the RIF, and populate those jobs with current employees that we wish to retain.

Easy, right? Well, I can tell you that I've lived this particular example a number of times and, no, it isn't! But it is simple.

Because all it takes is a Sponsor-level decision up-front as to whether people are interviewing for the new positions, or are being selected by some other methodology (e.g. talent selection committee). There is a secondary guiding principle/rule as to whether below-expectations employees will be considered.

Now, with those two things in hand, we can design the process quickly and easily…

Well, that's not my experience! You see, gather any group of HR professionals together to design this particular process and I guarantee you'll end up in lengthy, vociferous debates about fairness, justice, the rights-and-wrongs of the RIF, etc. You may even get a very well-intentioned set of recommendations to the CEO on how the RIF could be avoided. In other words, you'll meet a whole heap of *Change What's Changing* intended to stave off the pain of involuntary terminations. None of which alter the fact that the RIF is decided, and involuntary terminations will happen; the need for a well-designed process is non-negotiable.

Now, needless to say, this is a strong example, but I've found similar in process design projects relating to compensation, benefits, promotions, succession planning and on, and on.

Remember, *Change What's Changing* is an avoidance tactic, driven from very real emotions, many of which you may well feel yourself.

Even in the most thorny cases, my approach is always to design the most robust process I can so that, once it's running, it won't compound the pain felt by participants.

Boiling the ocean

Oh, how HR just loves to play this game!

In *Boiling The Ocean*, the process slated for design/redesign is lined up, and everyone is in vociferous agreement that it's a great piece of work to do. So good, in fact, that we should handle <*insert ancillary process here*> at the same time.

Before you know it, the single process design that was a) manageable; and b) cleared for take-off, is now bloated and bogged down in political infighting and quicksand.

The challenge here is that the resistance is a wolf in sheep's clothing - because it's cloaked in positivity.

Listen carefully for *"that's a great idea! Could we also…"* type conversations - they're a real warning sign. The greatest risk for you as a process designer is that there is an element of flattery involved here - people just LOVE that you're going to be designing the process, and they'd LOVE to have your amazing expertise deployed to their process, you'd be AMAZING…

Like I say, watch out for wolves in sheep's clothing…

Defending the current state

This resistance almost speaks for itself, and it's rife in HR, because of everything we discussed earlier in the book. This one IS the voice of the *status quo*!

The game here is for the resistor to avoid coming clean with a *"but I don't want things to change"* admission; that would never do!

Instead, the tactic is to vigorously explain the rationale and design decisions that went into the prior process design(s). This may even include discussing who was involved; it's always fun to hear people argue on behalf of people who have long since retired or left the company; it can sound like you're daring to rip down an historic monument!

In effect, this is an avoidance tactic, trying to rake over (sometimes ancient) history. Let the past be the past, but keep moving forwards.

Over involvement

This resistance has very overt, visible actions in the form of stuffing the process design team with representatives for different factions.

"We need an HR Business Partner from each division on the team…"

"Is recruiting represented?"

"What about a front-line supervisor?"

"Make sure IT is in the room…"

Before you know it, the team is 4 or 5 times as big as it needs to be and all those extra members aren't doing anything to design the process, but instead are slowing things down, and vociferously describing how the new process won't work for their group(s). Quite often, they'll be giving voice to the other resistances we've already covered.

And, of course, the notion of involvement is a good thing - we definitely want the process to work. But for design, involvement does not necessarily guarantee optimum outcomes.

Later we'll talk about how to involve people responsibly without compromising deliverables. For now, make sure your Sponsor is ready to back you up, then handle the inevitable involvement requests with a *"no thanks, the team is all set…"*

Designing to protect

There's nothing worse than a process that is sub-optimal simply because it's been designed around a person, role or function. In essence, we're back to a red flag we spoke about earlier in the book:

ARE YOU INVOLVED BECAUSE YOU'RE JUSTIFIED... OR JUSTIFIED BECAUSE YOU'RE INVOLVED?

But there's an added spin here, in that the process is actually assuming the involvement of a person, role or function in the future state.

Most often this happens because the process owner/deliverer is involved directly in design, and thus a subtle, unspoken *"sacred cow"* is brought into the room: *avoidance of job loss.*

There are occasions, however, where the current process owner doesn't fear for their job, but instead, can't conceive of a process running where they are not involved.

A number of years ago, early in my career, I redesigned our in-house relocation process to speed up expense reimbursements and reduce unnecessary signatures/approvals.

The relocation administrator was a highly competent professional who practiced a very loving and supportive touch with those relocating. In the early stages of the redesign, she just could not discuss how to reduce approval steps without equating it to *"not being able to talk to them"* and her underlying fear that people wouldn't be happy/supported.

As a result, every suggested refinement of process had to be exhaustively described and ring-fenced so it didn't impede her ability to be the *"face"* of relocation; and the proposed process actually grew more cumbersome.

As this became apparent, we had to pull in our Sponsor, who also happened to be her boss, to make clear his expectation that the process would be simplified and shortened; he also worked with the Relocation Administrator to set clear objectives around reduction in relocation workload in order to focus on other priorities (there was, as always in HR, more than enough other work to do).

In handling this resistance, going back to the original charter of process redesign: *"a fit-for-purpose process will be designed…"* is always a good thing.

Getting the plane off-the-ground

Given the sources of resistance we've just discussed, it's no surprise that many approach process design either as a black-box (i.e. *"I'll just go and get it done without telling anyone"*) or as a pointless quest.

I suggest you choose neither of these options!

Regardless of the resistance, we have scope and sponsor, which gives us the authority to act, and we know that, beyond those resistant stakeholders/participants, the world is aching for HR to make things more simple, helpful and productive.

Remember, resistance is loud and support often quieter.

Time to get ready for take-off!

DESIGNING THE PROCESS

And so we arrive at the meat and potatoes of designing a process - seriously... well done for getting this far!

This chapter is going to be very functional; think of it as the *what* and *how* of process design - though both of those are lower-cased, and we're going to be graduating to their bigger siblings in the next chapter.

But more on that when we get to it.

We've already broken down a process into 4 fundamental building blocks:

- Information
- Actions
- Decisions
- Roles

In this chapter, we're going to take these building blocks and begin to put them together.

To do this, we're going to use a very basic process as a working example: *what do we do when an employee wants to learn something.*

I've worded that very specifically as a needs-based statement, and I would encourage you to always do so, because HR too often starts from what's set in stone; in this case, Learning Management.

If our aim is to simplify processes, eliminate unnecessary steps, and focus on outcomes, we should be aiming for what we're being asked to do and not what we've already been doing.

Other examples might be:

- *A new hire wants to work virtually to the end of the school year…* vs. *Relocation Administration*
- *I want to care for my sick parent…* vs. *Benefits Elections*
- *I want to introduce a bonus system for my team…* vs. *Compensation Management*

This is far from exhaustive, but instead designed to give you a flavor. Starting process design from the right hand side (Relocation, Benefits, Compensation, etc.) could be more than is actually necessary, and maybe even miss the need that's being expressed.

So with that said, now let's break down process design into four handy-dandy sub-sections:

- WHY
- WHAT
- WHO
- HOW

WHY we are doing the process

We've already covered a lot of ground on the *"for the sake of what?"* of our process, and we're not going to retread those steps here. Instead, we are going inside the process and asking why we have a process at all.

And the answer is quite simple: *to make something happen.*

Remember our definition of a process:

> A PROCESS IS A CONSISTENT, REPEATABLE SERIES OF STEPS TOWARDS A CLEARLY-DEFINED END-POINT

So, our WHY becomes that end-point; that is to say the outcome(s) of the process. If we don't need an outcome, we don't need a process.

And while we're at it, we really should specify just what it is that causes the process to begin.

Let's introduce our first process mapping terms:

START-POINT: *The event, action or decision that triggers the process.*

END-POINT: *How we know that the process is complete.*

That's easy, right? Well, yes… And no. You would be surprised how many HR processes don't have a clearly defined Start- and End-point.

Start-point

In our example process, let's go right to our problem statement:

AN EMPLOYEE WANTS TO LEARN SOMETHING

That's a great start point. Very clear and concise; we have an employee, and that employee wants to learn something. Clear, huh?

Not so fast. Let's take a look at this statement from the vantage point of our 4 building blocks.

Is this information? Well, technically yes… But where is it resident? Where has it been activated? At the moment we have unactivated, undirected information - in other words, it's a data point, not a process building block.

Is this an action? Absolutely not. There's just no agency to it; it's just sitting there, an amorphous awareness at best.

Is this a decision? Nope.

Is this a role? Well, it's an employee, but that's about all we can say.

Now, as I described earlier, I chose this example because I wanted simplicity to be able to make simple points. And this is one of those occasions.

Just because someone wants to do something, doesn't mean there is, or should be, a process to help them do it.

Now, I know you're feeling short-changed by that, so let's keep digging on our Start-point.

Earlier in the book we discussed how much alignment is necessary. One way to think of processes is that one process always leads to another. The job ad process, leads to the interview process; the interview process to the hiring decision, to the offer process, to the onboarding process, and on, and on. We might think that *"Manager needs to fill job"* is the absolute starting point. And yet that need to fill a vacancy may be due to annual growth forecasts (a result of the budgeting process) or due to voluntary termination (a result of the resignation process) or due to any number of other processes.

The point is that, when designing a process, it's really important to clarify your Start-point in terms of what might cause it. Now, typically, this is going to reside in the final step of a previous process and is highly likely to be a decision or action.

There's an outside chance that it's a piece of information - and in the world of HRIS, then information flowing to a new gateway may trigger a process. I would argue, in this case, that the information is a system-coded form of a decision or action. Now that may feel like semantics, and to some extent it is, but if you ever step into the world of integrated systems, knowing this is really, really important.

Regardless, we can now ask the question: *"Which decision or action triggers our process?"*

For our employee who wants to learn something, we might imagine an annual development review flagging a learning need. A corrective performance plan might have identified a remedial aspect of learning. Accelerated talent and succession planning might have stretched the boundaries of the employee's current role, forcing them to run to catch up.

It doesn't really matter which process caused it; for our process Start-point, all we need to know is that:

AN EMPLOYEE IDENTIFIES A DEVELOPMENT NEED

Let's break it down once again.

Information - Not so much now; the Start-point isn't a piece of information flow or data.

Action - "... *identifies*..." reflects a present-tense, point-in-time action, even though we know that some other process has led to this point.

Decision - "... *a development need*..." reflects that a decision has been made to pursue specific development.

Role - it's still with the employee, for sure.

Look at them side by side:

AN EMPLOYEE WANTS TO LEARN SOMETHING	AN EMPLOYEE IDENTIFIES A DEVELOPMENT NEED

We've gone from an amorphous statement of awareness, to a specific, point-in-time, present-tense action. Our process can start!

START-POINT: AN EMPLOYEE IDENTIFIES A DEVELOPMENT NEED

Now, let's turn our attention to the other end of the process.

End-point

How will we know when the process is done? We know our statement of need: *An employee wants to learn something*. And we've tightened that up to more rigorous Start-point: *An employee identifies a development need*.

So, our End-point is easy, right? An employee learns something...

Well, we're bumping into the same thing as we did with the Start-point - that's a whole lot of amorphous, undirected stuff right there.

Learns what? Learns how? Learns where? When is the learning complete? Who delivers the learning? What was the learning meant to address anyway?

That's just 15 seconds of asking questions of this suggested End-point and the answers are infinite!

So, given that a single process that tries to map the universe of learning possibilities for each unique individual employee might be a little difficult to pull off, let's practice the *art-of-the-doable* and define a reasonable process end point that isn't just *"employee learns something"*.

Let's try this then: *Employee identifies developmental solution*.

It's an action, for sure, but is it a decision? What if the developmental solution is a 6-month sabbatical on a private estate on Bali. The process End-point will have been reached but the business case... not so much!

So, let's pull the camera back a bit and consider what the output of our process is for whichever process follows. In our particular example, it's the developmental solution that will deliver the learning.

With that in mind, for our process to have completed fully, the employee in question will start the learning process. So let's be blunt about the End-point:

END-POINT: EMPLOYEE COMMENCES DEVELOPMENTAL SOLUTION(S)

Now, the scope of our process feels more robust, like it's got a real start and end. We can think of it as a story: *Once upon a time, there was an employee who identified a development need… Some stuff happened… and the employee started developing…*

Like all good fiction writers, we don't know all the stuff in the middle (yet) but we know the journey we want our employee to complete.

Critical Success Factors

Let's go back to our Bali example, because it suggests we might be missing a word in our End-point: *appropriate* - i.e. an *"appropriate developmental solution."*

In the old school, HR more-often-than-not played the role of gatekeeper for the bureaucracy. And, in that old school, for sure, the word appropriate - or authorized, or approved, or designated, or assigned - would almost certainly have been part of the End-point. Unless you've been living under a rock, you know that those days are long in the rear-view mirror.

Here we hit a core guiding principle of HR process design - if I were into etching things on tablets of stone, this would be right up there on the list:

DO NOT REPLACE ACCOUNTABILITY WITH PROCESS STEPS

In our example, it's not enough that the employee has started their developmental solution, it must also be an appropriate solution. And somebody has to be accountable for making a judgement of what is appropriate, and that somebody should not be an HR rule-set.

Let's consider our example, it's highly likely that the employee's chain of command will make the decision on all aspects of the developmental solution; time to attend, budget, job adjustments, etc. All of which can be summarized in a simple statement: *Manager approves developmental solution(s)*.

And so we come to the notion of Critical Success Factors: those things that indicate the process has been completed satisfactorily. Formally stated:

Critical Success Factors: *A small number of performance measures that indicate the process has been fully completed for key stakeholder(s)*

Said differently, if we want to say the process checked all the boxes, then the Critical Success Factors, alongside a clear Start- and End-point, *are* the boxes.

As an aside, your End-point is a Critical Success Factor in-and-of-itself - i.e. if we don't reach the End-point, the process isn't a success!

A Critical Success Factor is something we look back on at the end of the process and ask did we meet that criterion? It's a yes or no question.

If it's no, then the process has not been designed fully - in this case, at minimum, it suggests we include a decision to approve on the part of the Manager (though it actually will mean more, but we'll get to that in good time!)

For now, we can add the following:

CRITICAL SUCCESS FACTOR: MANAGER APPROVES DEVELOPMENTAL SOLUTION(S)

Before we move onto the meat of actually designing the process, let's pause and consider something I've been adding to the main points above.

A quick note on fuzziness

Remember when we talked about mapping the ocean and boiling it? One of the ways that plays out in process design is demanding all the answers out of the gate.

"Come on!" the skeptic cries, *"If you don't know everything, how can you do anything?!"*

Don't interpret that for anything other than what it is: *a diversionary tactic*. It's impossible to start a process design project with the process already mapped. If you could, then you wouldn't need to do the work; and you've already got the sponsorship to do the work, therefore the process isn't designed.

Got it?

Good, because I'd like to introduce you to the notion of fuzziness. As I use the term, it's the transparent acknowledgement that we don't know everything, but we are open to learning more.

In our example above, I've introduced a little fuzziness in terms of the End-point. Did you notice?

Without telling you, I went from a discussion of an employee commencing a developmental solution to an End-point of *Employee commences developmental solution(s)*.

A couple of things happen here - the first is present-tense specificity (which will make sense once we get a little further in this chapter), the second is the deliberate fuzziness that there may be more than one developmental solution in play.

At some point, we may be forced to consider whether we drive a singular solution or not, but at this point in the design work, by leaving it fuzzy, we don't design towards a pre-ordained conclusion.

If I were a betting man - and seeing as how I'm writing the book, I'm getting pretty good odds - I suspect that the decision on singular or multiple solutions will end up in the Manager's approval step that we covered under Critical Success Factors, but the beauty of fuzziness is that we don't need to know that in order to get started.

Other examples?

Is it a reward process, or is it a recognition process? Don't know, we'll discover that along the way!

Is it internal posting or promotion? Don't know, let's work that out!

Who owns this process? Let's see where it makes sense to house the process after we've designed it!

This isn't avoidance or denial, it's deliberate fuzziness - and it's a really, really useful skill to have when designing HR processes in the face of a stodgy *status quo*.

So, we know where we're beginning (Start-point), we know where we want to get to (End-point), and we know how we'll know we've got there (Critical Success Factors).

Now we need to ask: *how do we get there?*

WHAT happens during this process?

Before we dive in to specifics, let's look at a simple example.

Let's say our plan is to travel from from the UK to the USA. It's easy to map that process right?

- Book tickets
- Pack bags
- Travel to airport
- Board plane
- Fly
- Land
- Clear immigration and customs

See how easy that was? Nothing to it really. But it can't really be that easy can it?

No, it can't! Let's look at why.

Key Assumptions

The first thing we have to know, understand and hold core is that:

> ### NO PROCESS EXISTS IN ISOLATION

This is really important for HR processes, where there are many interdependencies - and we'll be talking more about that a little later on - but there is a critical aspect of connection that we must keep in mind: *Key Assumptions*.

> ### KEY ASSUMPTION: A FACTOR OR CONDITION THAT MUST BE IN PLACE EXTERNAL TO THE STEPS DETAILED IN THE PROCESS

For the design of a process, we have to start with a line of sight on what needs to be in place in order for the process to function. If Critical Success Factors are how we look back on our process, Key Assumptions need to be in place before we even start.

In our US-trip example, here are just a few of the Key Assumptions that immediately come to mind:

- We have funds to pay for the ticket
- Ticket purchase mechanisms are in place
- Purpose of trip is defined (to enable packing)
- Air travel has been invented
- We have a passport

Now, some of these are pretty basic - and I use the example to illustrate that defining Key Assumptions can have a tendency to get out of hand!

Scope it out

One way to approach this is through a question of scope. In our example, the scope is simply to travel from the UK to the USA. It doesn't mention anything about a return trip. Nor does it speak to purpose of travel. And finally, it doesn't mention anything about where the traveler is in the UK; or indeed, who the traveler is!

Our scope is actually very limited and, using our framing:

Process Start-point: Leaves UK

Process End-point: Arrives USA

Critical Success Factor: Arrives USA

If this is our simplest statement of scope, then there is really only one Key Assumption:

- Trans-Atlantic travel is possible

What's especially clever about this Key Assumption is that it covers several fronts: 1) the method of travel - i.e. air, shipping, etc.; 2) Booking and ticket purchase; and 3) Customs and Immigration issues - i.e. passports.

By stating that Trans-Atlantic travel is possible, *we don't have to design it into our process.*

I'm going to press pause for a moment, right here because... Well... That's a really big deal. In fact, I don't think I typed it big enough, so let's try stating it as a guiding principle

WE DON'T HAVE TO DESIGN EVERYTHING INTO OUR PROCESS

Why is this so important to note? Because it's part of the antidote for the *Boil The Ocean* game. By making it clear that we assume something is in place, we don't have to design in actions and decisions to make sure it is. In practical terms, when a team member, subject matter expert or other stakeholder plays the Boil The Ocean gotcha game, you can pivot the conversation away from *"stop designing the process"* and instead towards *"how do we capture that as a Key Assumption?"*

When working through a process design, we might find that we don't know all the Key Assumptions when we begin. That's fine, it just presents us with another chance to be purposefully fuzzy!

In practice, this looks like a list of Key Assumptions that will be kept live throughout the design process, and added to, edited, or shortened based on decisions we make on individual process steps.

Let's circle back to our core example with the same approach to Key Assumptions. So far, we know that:

Process Start-point: Employee identifies a development need

Process End-point: Employee commences developmental solution(s)

Critical Success Factor: Manager approves developmental solution(s)

Once again, we could make a long-list of assumptions here - that the Manager and Employee are having regular performance and development discussions, that development budget exists, that workload is at a level that will allow employee to attend developmental activities, that the employee isn't in a formal disciplinary process... The list could go on and on, for sure.

But, once again, we can cut to the bone here based on scope, and then use our newly-learned fuzziness to keep an open mind.

Using that approach, there's really only one Key Assumption that we need make going in:

- Developmental solution(s) are available

As we walk through our process design, we'll expand on that bullet but, for now, it's enough to say that the process will undoubtedly break without the availability of developmental solution(s).

And, with that in hand, we're ready to start designing!

A Quick Note on Instincts

I want to take a moment to reflect on what just happened there - i.e. that in the space of a couple of paragraphs I took a host of complexity and boiled it down to 4 words. I did similarly in the Critical Success Factors section. Doing so feels obvious to me but, as my colleague Jo Short always reminded me, I take for granted things I already know and can do. All I can say is that, the more you design processes, the more you'll gain the experience and instincts to cut to the chase. There's also an element of bullishness here or, said differently, being willfully bullish. All of those potential Key Assumptions above are important, so it takes some strength to say *"I know, but let's not use them at the moment"*. As you'll see, it makes much more sense to start from the minimal case and then build out, rather than the other way around.

Starting simple

If you haven't guessed by now, I'm a strong advocate for KISS principles (Keep It Simple, Stupid). And so it goes with process design.

Before we get way, way down in the weeds, let's start this thing as simply as possible by deliberately pulling the camera back to the highest level, we'll then gradually increase our level of focus and granularity until the process is fully designed.

To do that, I want to introduce you to my favorite process design tool. It isn't software, it isn't complex algorithms, it isn't even a graphical user interface. It's a *Post-It®* note, plain and simple!

I love *Post-it®* notes for many tasks, but for process design, they are indispensable. Each one represents a process step and, can be quickly arranged and rearranged on a wall or white-board to see what the best flow is.

I'll represent a note by this symbol:

[Note]

Let's start with our Start- and End-points:

[Employee identifies development need] → [Employee commences development solution(s)]

Great, we have a process - it's that arrow!

Now, we just have to work out what happens to make that process work, so we can begin to focus in - I'll go through it in steps to illustrate, but you probably won't find it as painstaking in real life. And, once you've done your first one, you'll be surprised how fast you can actually get this stage done.

The first step is to add anything we specifically know about the process already.

For instance, we know that the Manager approval is a Critical Success Factor, so let's add a simple "Approve…" step:

[Employee identifies development need] → [Approve development solution(s)] → [Employee commences development solution(s)]

And this is where this early, simple approach comes into its own. We simply have to ask good questions, such as: *"What has to happen in order for the solution to be approved?"*

Well, that kind of assumes that someone has already identified potential a development solution(s) that will meet the need, doesn't it?

This has to happen before the approval step, so at the highest level, our simple *Post-It®* process becomes:

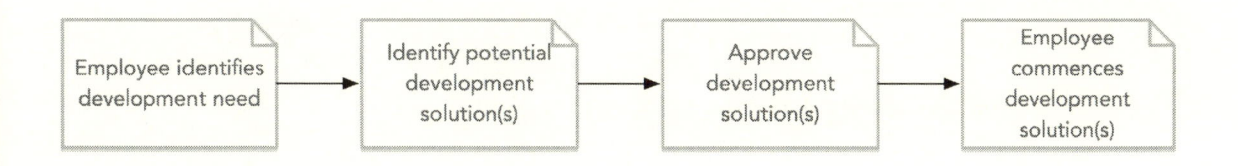

```
[Employee identifies development need] → [Identify potential development solution(s)] → [Approve development solution(s)] → [Employee commences development solution(s)]
```

There are a couple of things to notice here.

Firstly, although we know that both Start- and End-points relate to the employee, we're NOT making any role assignments to the internal process steps at the moment. We don't want to pre-guess the process, and will get to roles soon enough.

The second thing to notice is that we haven't tried to go deep down into the weeds of the process yet, we've deliberately kept it high level, so that it meets the KISS principle.

Put simply, these 4 steps make sense and, as we focus in, we'll expand each of them in a similar way. Remember we are trying to avoid unnecessary complexity, not introduce it!

Let's expand the process a little further by adding some more *Post-it*® notes...

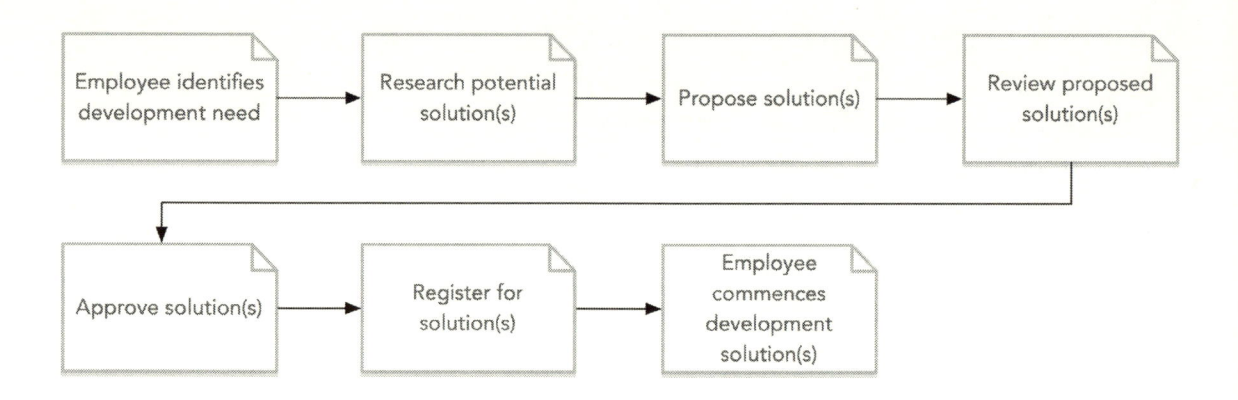

```
[Employee identifies    →   [Research potential   →   [Propose solution(s)]   →   [Review proposed
 development need]         solution(s)]                                              solution(s)]
                                                                                         ↓
[Approve solution(s)]   →   [Register for         →   [Employee commences
                             solution(s)]              development
                                                       solution(s)]
```

Although this is on two rows, we're still talking about a linear process flow here, just follow the arrows!

Walking through this process, we can already see three of our building blocks in play:

- **Information** - *Research potential solution(s)*
- **Actions** - *Propose solution(s)*
- **Decisions** - *Approve solution(s)*

Could we go further in defining the linear process at this point? Possibly, although we're getting very close to having to consider roles.

For example, who provides the information on potential solutions? Who is involved in the approval process, and how does it work? How does the registration work, and who does it?

When you have your linear process to the granularity where the obvious next questions are about roles, it's time to start swimming!

WHO is involved in the process?

Let's introduce the construct of swim-lanes. These are singular to each role involved in a process, though sometimes actions overlap swim-lanes - we'll talk more about that when we look at HOW the process works.

For now, let's ask the question: *who might be involved in this process?* The first two roles should be obvious because they're directly connected to the Start- and End-points and Critical Success Factors:

- Employee
- Manager

Assuming we're not a one-person HR function, we may add the following to the list:

- Learning & Development Function
- External Learning Providers

We might also add specific systems:

- Learning Management System (LMS)
- Training Course Registration

For now, I'm not going to add individual systems as roles, and instead indicate them as integration points within the Learning & Development Function swim-lane.

Welcome to the machine

As an aside, in complex processes, particularly those closely integrated with HRIS, I like to provide a swim-lane specifically for the system - i.e. treat it as a role within the process. Over time, you'll develop a gut feel for when it's appropriate to do this, and when to do so would be a case of overkill.

So, with that said, we can take a view of our prototype swim-lanes:

[Swim-lane diagram with four empty horizontal lanes labelled (top to bottom): External Providers, L&D Function, Manager, Employee]

Hopefully, it's clear why we call them swim-lanes? The process will run like a one-length swimming race, with each role swimming from left to right. I have seen swim-lanes produced vertically - and if you work in an organization that tends to print out portrait documents, that can work well - however I prefer landscape, left-to-right. As always, do what works for you, just be consistent!

Our next step is to populate the swim-lanes with our *Post-It®* notes.

Depending on how you're designing the process - as an individual or a team - you may actually want to do this physically on a wall so you can see the whole flow.

In a global process alignment project I led, we literally put 5 flip-chart pages along a wall and drew our swim-lanes, then positioned the *Post-It®* notes where they went. We were then able to debate each *Post-It®* as to who should do it, and how it flowed - literally picking up the note and moving it on the wall. It was a great team exercise, and totally appropriate for what were very complex processes, and particularly useful in identifying where we were able to gain efficiencies by having steps run parallel to each other.

Here are the swim-lanes populated with our simple *Post-It®* process:

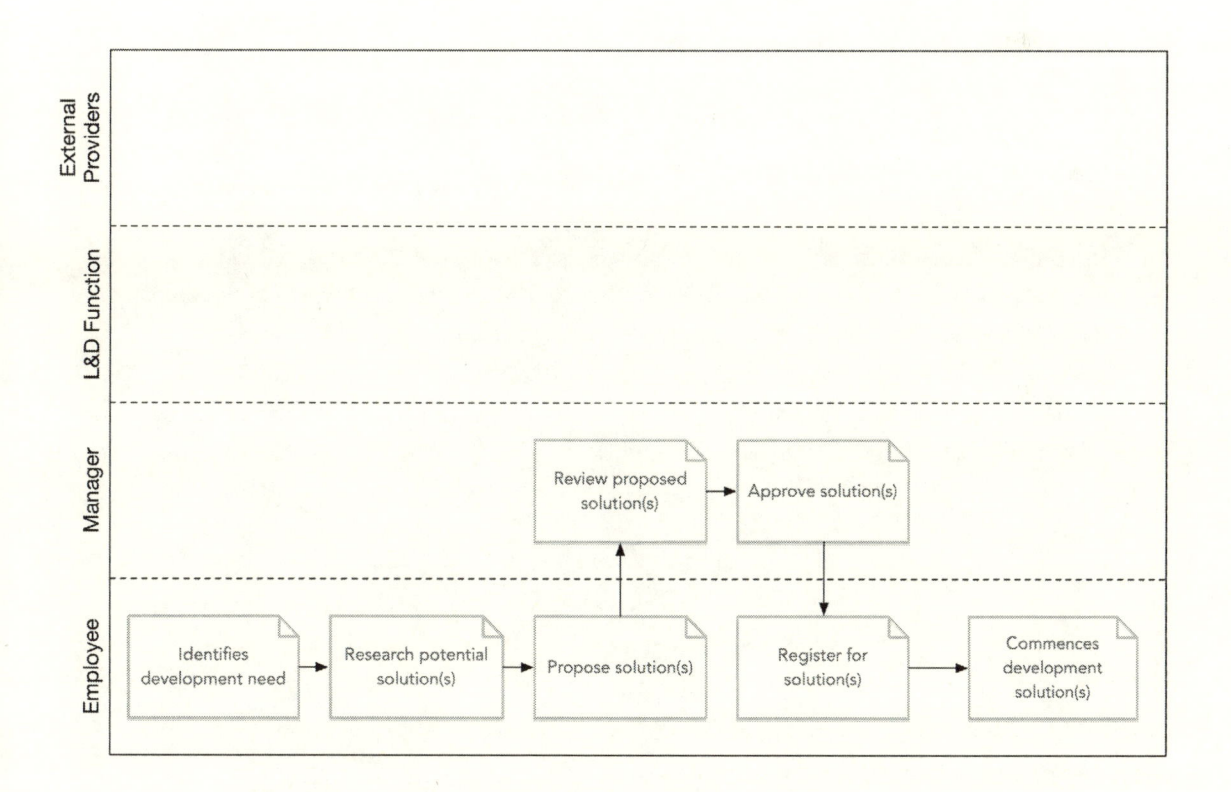

External Providers	
L&D Function	
Manager	Review proposed solution(s) → Approve solution(s)
Employee	Identifies development need → Research potential solution(s) → Propose solution(s) → Register for solution(s) → Commences development solution(s)

There, that was easy! Take a look at the flow.

It's really clear what the Employee needs to do, and when the Manager gets involved. Though it has to be said that it looks like L&D and the External Providers got off easy, doesn't it?

Well, not so much - but we'll get to that in a moment, although it's worth noting that, if you do meet a situation where a swim-lane has few steps, or even none, it's worth asking if the swim-lane can be eliminated completely.

Next we'll provide more specific detail on the *Information*, *Actions* and *Decisions* that have been summarized with a *Post-It®*.

Before we do that however, once we have our *Post-It®* flow in swim-lanes, I like to come *"off-note"* and move into software - this provides much more flexibility for editing and transfer of flow diagrams into other media.

Use what works

I won't recommend specific software for process design, though I do encourage you to use specific process-mapping packages and to avoid using more generic solutions such as PowerPoint, Keynote, etc. (and definitely, definitely not Word or Excel!)

Process diagrams throughout the book have been produced using OmniGraffle Pro for Mac OS X - if I were in Windows, I would be very likely be using Microsoft Visio.

Graphically speaking, there are any number of process design norms in terms of what shape means what. I don't tend to get too hung up on conforming to any single framework (remember, *Questioning The Method* is one of the key resistance plays) and the only time that I find it really becomes important is when working cross-functionally, particularly when specifying the human process that touches information systems. In such process design work, making sure that the left- and right- hands of the organization share a common language is critical.

> For the purposes of our journey in this book, we'll follow some internal consistency - i.e. we'll use the same shape for the same building block throughout the book - and that's all you really need to do in your own process design.
>
> Rather than do a long reference list of shapes and symbols here, I'll provide a glossary for reference at the end of the book. For now, I'll point out new shapes when they appear, so that I can describe their use.

A software generated version of our process flow looks like this:

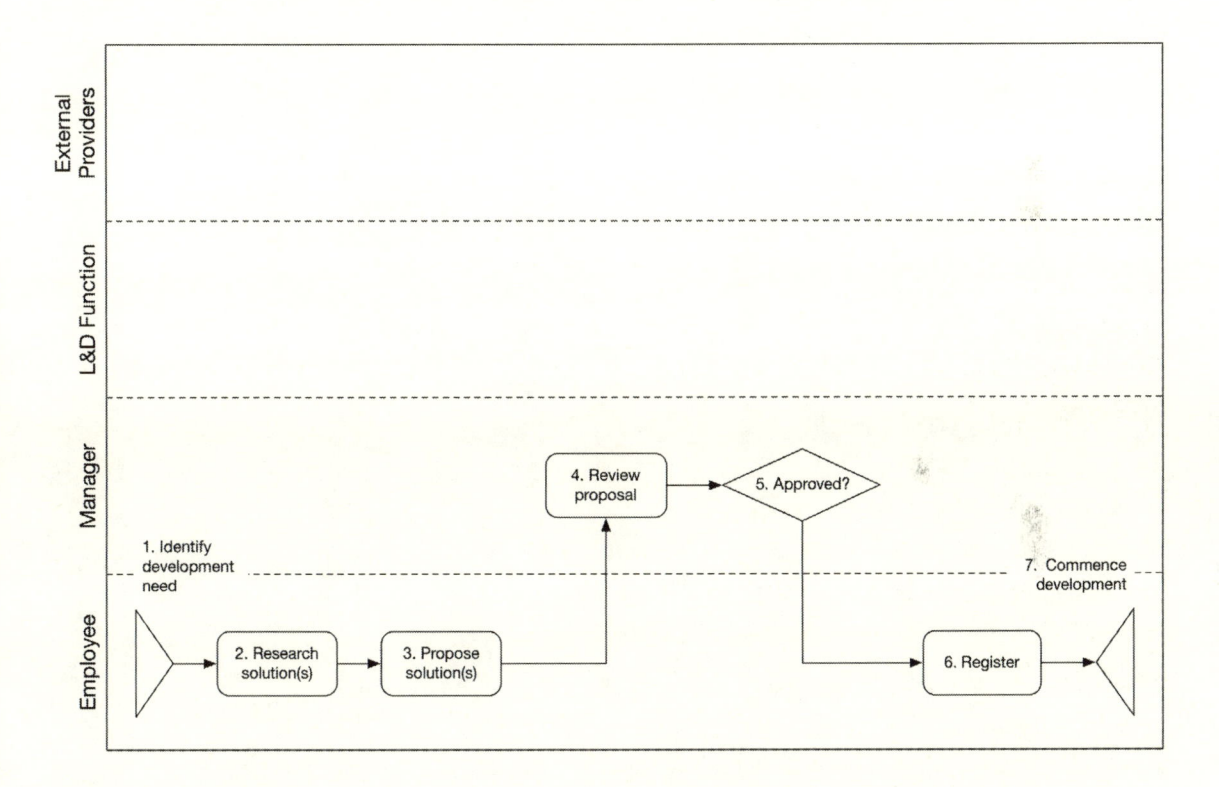

[Process flow diagram with swimlanes: External Providers, L&D Function, Manager, Employee. Steps: 1. Identify development need → 2. Research solution(s) → 3. Propose solution(s) → 4. Review proposal → 5. Approved? → 6. Register → 7. Commence development]

A few things to point out here, not least of which how much cleaner it looks!

Firstly, I've numbered each step, the reason for which will become apparent very soon.

I've clearly identified the *Start-* and *End-points*. These are not action steps, so they aren't indicated as such. I like to use the left and right triangles as they have a sense of visually book-ending the process.

So far, I haven't indicated specific *Information* sources or flows.

I have indicated *Actions* with a rounded rectangle - for now, we'll treat them as singular actions though, in a little while, I'll show you how they can provide a placeholder for multiple actions or sub-processes.

I've indicated *Decisions* with a diamond, as I mentioned a moment ago. A *Decision* differs from an *Action* because it is a point in time and has a specific, directive effect - in this case, to lead to *6. Register*.

Finally, because we have specified our swim-lanes and the flow is in action, we can really simplify the language used on the diagram. For example *"Approves proposed development solution(s)"* becomes a simple *Decision* diamond: *5. Approved?*

Taken together, this provides a very clean flow-chart for our simple example process.

That said, do you notice a break-down?

What happens if the Manager does NOT approve the request? By placing a *Decision* diamond on the chart, we have to now account for all possibilities emerging from that *Decision*, so let's provide a route for that...

To do this, we'll make the decision point absolute - i.e. a *"yes"* or a *"no"*. I hope I don't need to say it, but we shouldn't encode *"maybe"* into our process flow!

Looking at *5. Approved?* we can see that, if it's a *"yes"*, then the process moves forward. If it's a *"no"* then the process loops back, asking the Employee to do more research before proposing alternatives.

In this instance, detailing the decision this way will ensure that the process meets its Critical Success Factor of Manager approval.

As an aside, we could have an alternative process End-point here if the Manager flat-out refuses to approve ANY development solution.

As the process is designed right now, we would be caught in an endless loop of research, proposal and non-approval. For simplicity's sake in this example, I've assumed that *"Do nothing"* would be the ultimate proposal in that scenario, and the Manager would approve that proposal. In more complex processes, it may be better to treat each potential decision point as its own sub-routine, particularly if there isn't a clear yes/no decision.

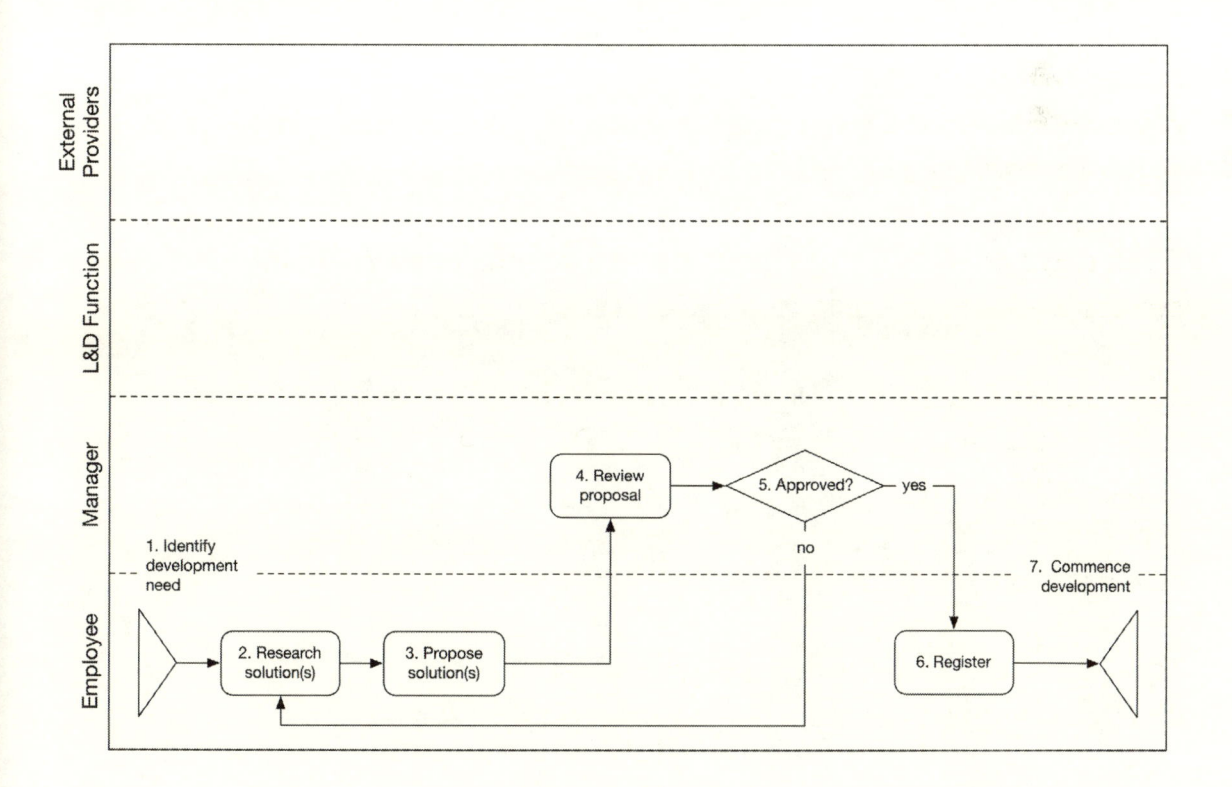

Now, having fleshed out the process, including the key decision, we're still left asking: *"but what about the other swim lanes?"* Let's take a look at that.

Let's focus on process *2. Research solution(s)* and ask: *"What has to be in place for the Employee to be able to research potential solutions?"*

Although that's a very a simple question, we might reasonably expect a varied and nuanced answer or, in the extreme, the equivalent of *Boiling The Ocean*. After all, our Employee potentially has the complete internet to research potential solutions! We must summarize.

As an example, let's completely eliminate one swim lane: *External Providers.*

Why so? Well, it comes back to that notion of scope. If we try to map everything that any or all External Provider(s) needs to do, we'll soon be into how they manage their vacation schedule, and back-up trainers, and all manner of other minutiae that we just shouldn't be mapping.

Remember when we discussed Key Assumptions and decided to be deliberately fuzzy? This is a good example of how that plays out.

We already have one Key Assumption: *"Development solutions are available"*? Well, we're going to add a couple of others to help manage this tightening of scope.

- Learning & Development function remains accountable for External Provider delivery[i]
- Latest information from External Providers, and registration mechanism, are available via Learning Management System (LMS)

---

[i] I try and avoid capturing functional accountability as a process step - in this case "Manages External Providers" - as it reads too much like "does job", but I'll keep it here in the assumptions because it acts as an indicator when we capture the process details

With these additional Key Assumptions, our process map becomes:

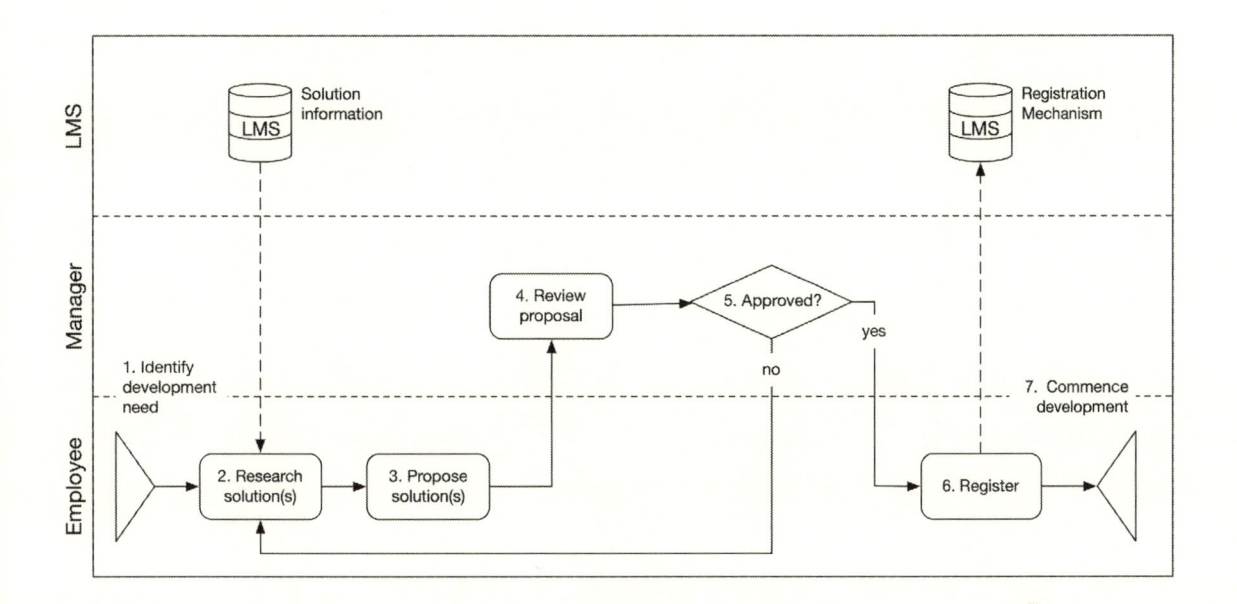

To my eyes at least, this looks like a streamlined process - easy-to-read and understand. We can see the expectations within each role, and how and when the information flows from data-stores (Solution Information), and to structured functionality (Registration).

Could we go more granular? Potentially. If we wanted to stipulate, for example, how the review and approval process takes place - whether templates are involved, etc. - we might want to do that. Here are a couple of examples of how that might look.

In the first, we're going to use a symbol to indicate that there is a sub-process at work, this is signified by a slight change to the symbol and wording of step 3. This double line indicator is a pretty common convention in process design and, when things become very complex, can be a useful approach to maintain focus upon the scope of the specific process in hand. Basically, this symbol says: *"several things happen here, before this process moves on."*

Here's what it looks like:

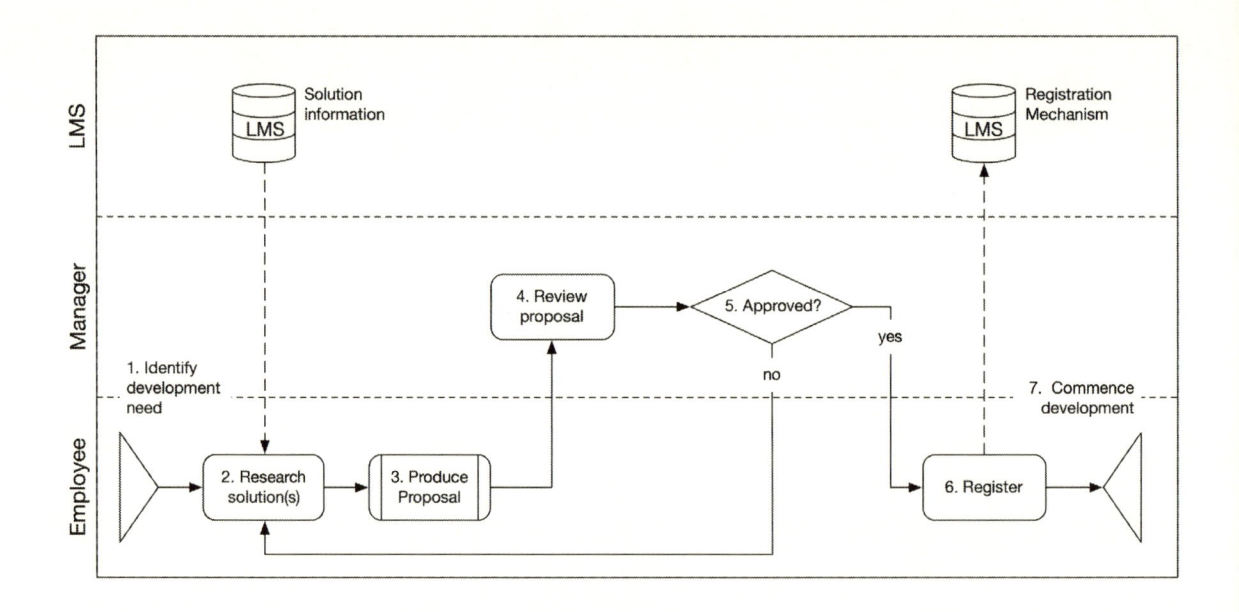

The second approach repositions steps 3, 4 and 5 with the direct implementation of the LMS as the proposal/approval mechanism:

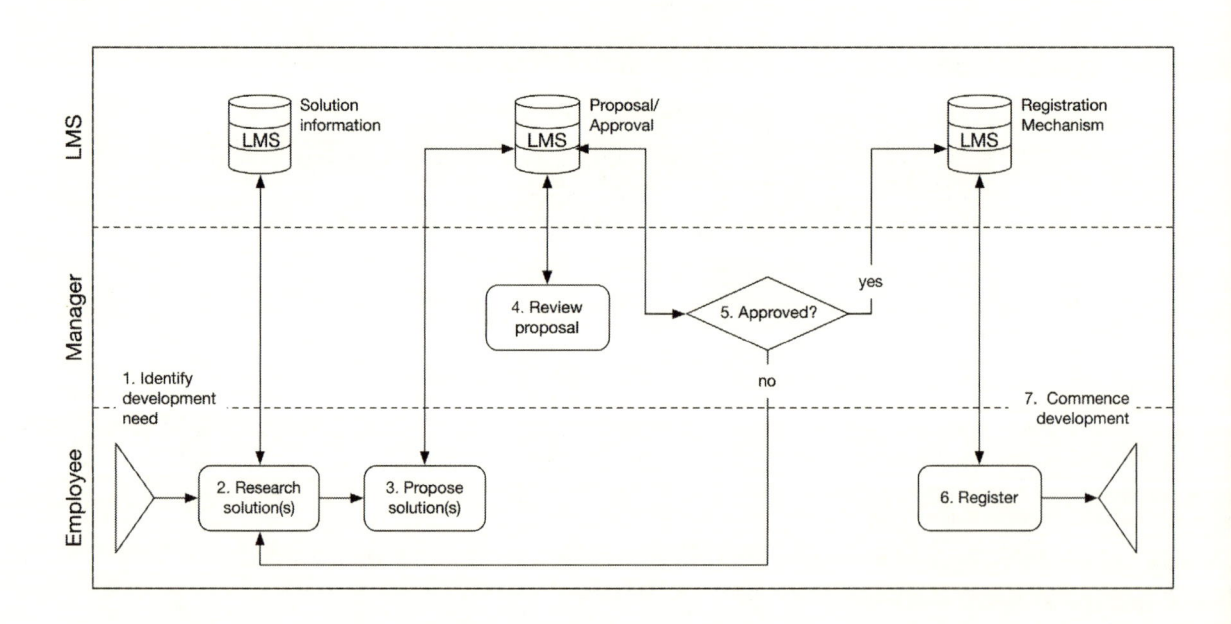

One thing to notice here, is that it's now clear that our top swim-lane isn't about the L&D Function any longer, and I've edited it to specifically call-out to the LMS - this is an example of where a system is treated as a role in the process.

By splitting out the approval process, the whole middle section of the flow has changed - blur your eyes a little and you'll see that the process map is now *"top-heavy"* where before it was *"bottom-heavy"* - it also looks more messy, with double headed arrows to indicate system interactions.

At minimum, by using this approach we've found that the capabilities resident within the LMS have become much more important.

I could actually argue that the LMS is moving from being a Key Assumption (owned and operated by Learning & Development), and maybe even going so far as becoming its very own Critical Success Factor in the second option (i.e. *"Development review and approval is completed via the LMS"*). This suggested change to our process might cause us to revisit Sponsorship and delegate the process design to L&D completely (if it were sitting elsewhere).

How granular do we go?

The answer to level of granularity of process design will, ultimately, be driven by the process itself.

If there is a need for formal tracking of decisions to protect against future legal challenges, then having a strict, robust process to achieve that is imperative, however how that is represented should be guided by the local legal framework.

At the other end of the spectrum, there may not even need to be a process for day-to-day decisions and actions; one reason HR is criticized for being bureaucratic.

For our example, I think we've gone deep enough in designing the process for illustrative purposes, particularly with those potential edits.

Before we move on, let's pull the camera back a little and see what we just did, because it highlights why process design is so much more valuable than simple efficiency and neatness.

By stating our initial Key Assumptions, we made it clear that when our employee identifies a development need, then L&D would be assumed to be the portal to solutions. That's not exactly an Earth-shattering insight - I did, after all, deliberately choose a simple example!

But let's say it wasn't such an obvious example. Let's say you were dealing with a recognition process that touched on developmental experiences. Is it still L&D, or is it under the Compensation function? How does it sit alongside the more holistic talent & succession planning processes?

This is where deliberate fuzziness of Key Assumptions can help flush out organization silos and sewers when it comes to processes. There's nothing quite like stating *"We assume <function X> will deliver <process factor Y> on time and to specification..."* to focus the attention of both the process designer AND function X!

In our example, if L&D doesn't deliver connection to external providers and a fit-for-purpose LMS, the process will be, at best, sub-optimal and, at worse, completely broken.

With our two alternative flows, we're actually going much further, and placing full delivery of functionality and content within the LMS, placing even more of an accountability target on the back of L&D.

The one thing we can't know right now is how this will play out in reality. We have, as described earlier, chosen to disconnect process design from process implementation for the moment.

For now, the key takeaway is this: *through process design we uncover the reality of potential change, reducing the likelihood of unexpected fire-fights once we reach implementation.*

> ### A note on legal frameworks
>
> If you haven't read my biography, you might not know that I'm a Brit living and working in the US. One of the things I learned very quickly is that the basis of employment law - specifically fair treatment - is fundamentally different on each side of the Atlantic. In the UK, if an employee or applicant brings a case of discrimination, the company is required to prove it did not discriminate (i.e. the company could be viewed as *"guilty until proven innocent"*), however in the US, the burden of proof is upon the Plaintiff (i.e. the company could be viewed as *"innocent until proven guilty"*).
>
> The net result of this is an impact on documentation standards. For example, in the UK, there is a strong focus upon disciplined note-taking and document storage. UK policy, procedure and guidelines are typically very detailed. In the US, however, the opposite is often the case, with policies reduced to single sentences, and significant concerns of document discoverability.
>
> What does this mean for process design? Be as detailed as you need to be to satisfy local legal expectation. If in doubt, consult with your employment law specialists.

HOW the process works

Towards the end of the last section, we patted ourselves on the back for designing the process:

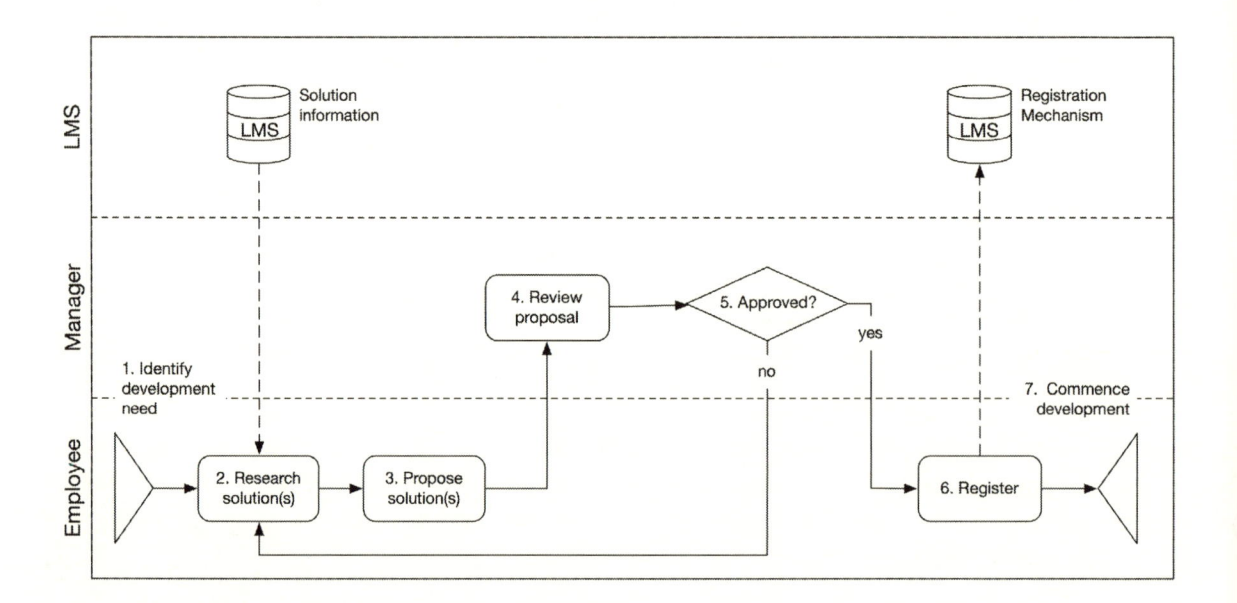

[Process flow diagram with swim lanes for LMS, Manager, and Employee showing steps: 1. Identify development need → 2. Research solution(s) → 3. Propose solution(s) → 4. Review proposal → 5. Approved? (no loops back to 2, yes continues) → 6. Register → 7. Commence development. LMS databases show "Solution information" and "Registration Mechanism".]

After all, we've successfully identified the steps as well as who takes them. A simple process, for sure, and not very much work to define.

I do note that, for many HR processes out there in the real world, this level of clarity is not readily available even though it's pretty simple to derive a flow like this.

Doing the job fully, though, requires us to go beyond the WHAT and WHO, and to fully define the HOW of the process.

Simply put, we have to detail each step, how it takes place and what it means.

The HOW is especially important in modern HR because of the multiple interfaces that may occur between the process and in-house HRIS as well as online B2B web-services.

To fully define the process, we're going to use two tools alongside each other:

- Process Narrative
- RACI Chart

Process Narrative

This is a long-form description of each process step, capturing the intent of the action/decision and any assumed data/information. For our process flow-chart above, the Process Narrative might look something like this:

ID	Stakeholder	Step	Description
1	Employee	Identify learning need	Employee identifies a learning need - this may occur during the normal course of working or (e.g.) as part of a developmental review.
2	Employee	Research solution(s)	Employee researches possible learning solutions within the Learning Management System, as well as external alternatives.
3	Employee	Propose solution(s)	Employee completes a learning proposal template and uses online work-flow to submit for Manager review.
4	Manager	Review proposal	Manager reviews learning proposal for fit with employee development aims, business objectives, time availability and budget.
5	Manager	Approved (Y/N)	Y - Manager communicates approval to Employee N - Manager communicates non-approval to Employee and agrees next step - either refreshed proposal or that no learning option will be approved
6	Employee	Register	Employee registers for approved learning solution(s) using Learning Management System registration, or external sign-up (as appropriate)

Hopefully, even though this is a very short process, you can see how describing each step in narrative form has introduced a whole heap of questions and ambiguity; the narrative has made things more complex!

Take a breath, that's by design…

By describing how the process will actually run, rather than the simple steps of the diagram, we've highlighted where we have potential break-down points, here are just a handful from this narrative alone:

- Step 1: Will there be an automated route to connect the formal development review to the identification of learning needs?
- Step 2: To what extent are external solutions likely to be approved? Is it a free-for-all in the *"Wild West"* of the internet, or are their preferred vendors?
- Step 3: Wait, there's a learning solution proposal template? And an online approval mechanism?!
- Step 4: What guidance does the Manager draw on to make this decision? What budget do they have? How does the Manager ensure equal treatment in learning compared with other employees?
- Step 5: Writing the narrative identified a potentially endless loop of non-approval/research & propose solutions, so we had to add a BIG non-approval (i.e. the whole thing is off-the-table).
- Just for fun, we also guided the Manager to communicate decision - is there a system-based route for that, maybe it's part of the one we uncovered in Step 3?
- Step 6: If the Employee signs up for an external provider, how will that be billed/paid?

And, undoubtedly, there will be more questions that emerge whenever we add detail to the narrative, which is precisely why we use this tool. As we iterate on the process narrative, we can begin to summarize some deliverables:

1. Approval workflow (inc. templates)
2. Employee Learning Guidelines
3. Learning Expense Policies & Procedures

By using the Process Narrative tool, we've got a better handle on HOW each step happens (and downstream implementation consequences of designing the process this way).

> ### What gets measured gets done
>
> A quick look at our example process shows few areas of measurable performance, however we might imagine that there were budgetary implications for development, and there may be an expectation of completion of process by an externally imposed deadline.
>
> Whatever measurable factor we do find associated with a process, the Process Narrative is a good place to capture it. In our example, this would bring some specificity to *4. Review Proposal* and we might imagine a turnaround time of approval, or completion deadlines in *5. Approved? (Y/N)*
>
> For more measurable, complex processes we might add a Key Performance Measures section to our Process Pack giving specific measures at each step - the recruitment process might be a good example of this - however for the purposes of the book, I'll limit myself to placing performance measures in the Process Narrative itself.

Before we consider the job done, though, we need to use the most powerful (and, when it comes to large/complex processes, often the most excruciating!) tool in process design: *the RACI Chart*.

Completing the RACI Chart

RACI stands for: *Responsible*, *Accountable*, *Consulted*, *Informed*.

For our purposes, these are defined as:

> *Responsible* - Completes the step directly or in collaboration with another
>
> *Accountable* - Has final approval for the step - the buck stops here
>
> *Consulted* - Provides information/input to the step
>
> *Informed* - is notified that the step is happening/has happened

For the purposes of clarity, we've been using a brief, simple process to illustrate design fundamentals - given that, using RACI will likely feel like overkill; but it's always good to start on something simple!

Here's what the RACI chart looks like for our process:

ID	Step	Employee	Manager	LMS
1	Identify learning need	RA	C	
2	Research solution(s)	RA		C
3	Propose solution(s)	RA	I	
4	Review proposal	C	RA	C
5	Approved (Y/N)	I	RA	
6	Register	RA		CI

With only 3 roles in this process, the RACI chart is pretty simple but it already highlighted something that we'd missed when drafting our linear process.

In *4. Review Proposal* let's ask the question: *How does the Manager assess the appropriateness of the development solution?*

Well, unless the Manager carries complete curriculum knowledge on them at all times, it's pretty clear they're going to have to review information somewhere. They may wish/need to consult the LMS, or even discuss the proposed solution with a member of Learning & Development.

Fast forward to implementation, and we've highlighted the need to ensure Manager view of potential solutions - does that sound like a Key Assumption? We already have:

- Latest information from External Providers, and registration mechanism, are available via Learning Management System (LMS)

So, we can probably get away with a slight tweak:

- Latest information from External Providers, and registration mechanism, are available to both Employees and Managers via Learning Management System (LMS)

This is one of the primary benefits of the RACI approach: it forces us to slow down and ask the right questions of each step.

Now, as I say, this is a very simple example process, but RACI really comes into its own when we work on more complex processes, as well as those loaded with organizational change implications.

And, as soon as we discuss change implications, we just know that resistance games are likely to appear. In my experience that is nowhere more true than during RACI charting, so let's take a look at some of the specific challenges you'll face, beginning with the *BIG A*!

RACI Challenge 1 - The Accountability Dodge

If you haven't noticed, most companies talk a really good game around accountability, but far fewer actually hold people fully accountable for their actions and results.

We work in organizations and teams where we have meetings to discuss meetings, many of which end up with minutes that try to describe a conversation, yet fail to capture agreements and, specifically, WHO will do WHAT as a result of the meeting.

Against this backdrop, RACI charting is a lot like a UV blacklight in a crime drama, highlighting the unseen forensic evidence of organization culture.

The first thing we see in the Accountability Dodge is having more than one column with an **A** in it. If this happens, challenge the notion right away.

When it comes to process design, we must hold the line at a single **A** per action.

I've heard this described in many ways, such as where the buck stops, who has final authorization, etc. but my favorite came in a global process re-engineering project, when one of our Subject Matter Experts, Monique, burst out laughing:

"OH, YOU MEAN *'WHO GETS WHACKED'*?"

To this day, I'm still not sure whether it was a reference to The Sopranos or The Godfather, or just to corporal punishment in general, but she was right. For any given step, **A** is the single person accountable for making sure it happens, and happens well, even if they're not the one taking the action directly.

This leads to the second aspect of the Accountability Dodge - a hypothetical game of escalating the Accountable ranking. The game is to imagine convoluted worst-case scenarios (often based on the *"blue sock clause"* I'll cover later in the book) for process steps that would force accountability to escalate up the organization.

Let's use an example from our simple process, and look at the approval step. Some well-intentioned soul in the design team asks: *what if the Manager makes a discriminatory approval decision?*

And, indeed, we haven't allowed for that in our process steps. In fact, this is an example of a fuzzy *Key Assumption* as we discussed earlier in the book - i.e. the Manager's ability to manage in a non-discriminatory way is a factor or condition that must be in place external to the steps detailed in the process.

Nevertheless, here we are in the design session and the whirlwind is spinning up.

Pretty soon, we've got to be protecting against legal challenge by ensuring any discoverable documents or records are retained, that the Manager has to get authorization from two levels above, that the Chief Legal Officer is on the hook and… No, screw that… If this goes all the way to trial, the CEO will be called to account to the Board and shareholders.

THE CEO IS ACCOUNTABLE! FOR EVERYTHING!

No, the CEO is not Accountable for the specific action of approving a development solution for an employee. See how unworkable that is?

Yet the game will be played. And, if not nipped in the bud, will play over and again as you go through the RACI charting exercise.

For this reason, I like to state up front the proviso that the Accountable party has to occupy a single swim-lane on the process flow; then, the first time the game starts, I explain the above and then suggest that the person who insists on playing the game go write the email to the CEO telling them that they have their own swim-lane on our little process and, as a result, are now Accountable for the specific process step in question. I do this with a smile and laugh, so that I can refer back to it whenever the game next starts up.

Make no mistake, when you see this, it's a subtle form of resistance to both the process design itself, and the tough questions that process design asks, but also a preemptive reaction to the implementation of any change resulting from a process redesign.

RACI Challenge 2 - Consult/Inform EVERYBODY!

Earlier in the book, we discussed HR process gate-keepers and a legacy attitude of value through involvement. To challenge this attitude, I shared this question:

ARE YOU INVOLVED BECAUSE YOU'RE JUSTIFIED... OR JUSTIFIED BECAUSE YOU'RE INVOLVED?

In RACI Challenge 2, we're going to see how this will come to life in our process design and what to do about it.

As we've already seen, for any process step, we have our Responsible party/parties - the people doing the step. One of our **R**'s may also be the Accountable party - though they may not.

We now need to detail who needs to provide input to the action step - i.e. be Consulted. And who needs to be Informed that the action is happening/has happened.

What we see in this challenge is a reversion to type for HR - particularly if redesigning an existing process.

You see, particularly in small HR groups, it can feel like *everybody* is involved in *everything*! So, when we design the process and we ask *"to make this step happen, who needs to be consulted?"* we'll get the answer we deserve: *EVERYONE!*

And we'll hear similar to this for who needs to be informed, though there will be an added wrinkle of not wanting to exclude people, particularly if the action comes anywhere near senior leadership.

If we don't catch this challenge, we can end up with rows full of **C** and **I** for every swim-lane; worse, we can see additional swim-lanes proposed solely to cater for this passive involvement.

Needless to say, adding unnecessary swim-lanes does not meet our desire to design a fit-for-purpose process!

There are three tricks to navigate this particular challenge and, as always, they come in the form of questions that can challenge the process design team's thinking:

1) What happens if they are not…?

This question applies to both Consulted and Informed. And, if the answer is that the step goes ahead without any change to it's effectiveness or efficiency, then you can pretty much assume that the **C/I** in question is on shaky ground.

Go through each one with a hard lens of *"tell me why we MUST include this **C/I**?"* and make your call as to whether to put it on the RACI chart or not. Either way, capture why you made that decision, so that you can explain it at any later stage in the process design project.

As a side-note here, the removal of legacy **C/I** elements from a process redesign can present a change implication - i.e. you may have to let people know that they will no longer be Consulted/Informed of process steps. Given that most people are way too busy, this is rarely a difficult sell; though to hear some HR colleagues, you might believe it's the end of the world! Either way capture your reasoning.

2) What are they going to do with it?

This is a way to pick apart endless Inform lists. Essentially we're using this question to identify the Inform party who actually *needs* to know something has happened because it will trigger/impact their own action.

Work through each **I** on the chart and ask *"what will this party do as a result of being informed?"* - if the answer isn't an action, then our Inform is likely to be a) an organizational politeness; or b) a legacy *"just because"*. Either way we can make the call as to whether we want to include it in the process RACI chart.

3) How do we empower them?

I'm old enough to remember a time when HR processes were delivered via paper and pen, and email only sparingly used to inform people of end results. Compared to those days we now live in times of abundant information interconnectivity.

This means two things for our overuse of **C/I** on the RACI chart and, once again, we're back to our guiding principle of ensuring human touch-points only where they add value to the process.

Firstly, we should be looking for systems to provide reference information wherever possible - this is such a simple aspect, and taken for granted in our cloud-based HRIS landscape, yet still we have processes that ask Managers to manually fill out details about their direct reports. Frankly, it's inexcusable to inject redundant actions into a process; an exercise in value-destruction, simply because we distract people from doing their job. In the US, it's similar to having to fill out your basic information every time you visit the doctor's office; frustrating!

Unfortunately, this is one of those places where the left-hand of HR doesn't know what the right-hand is doing. It occurs because we tend to spend our time in our own corner of the HRIS ecosystem - if we're in compensation, we're in the reward modules, talent acquisition in the ATS, etc. And, sadly, HR business partners not really using the system too deeply at all - maybe even using shadow system spreadsheets maintained by their clients.

Fixing this is beyond the purview of this book, but knowing that it can lead to process inefficiencies is really important; process design is one of the best places to call out such behavior, simply by asking the right questions.

These opportunities to call out, and enable, system solutions nearly always show up in discussions of the Inform role, though there can also be an unhealthy dose of organizational politics involved as well. HR has historically protected itself from repercussions by involving stakeholders in everything. This is, of course, a wasteful strategy - particularly because it often really annoys those stakeholders.

In this history, HR has taken a *PUSH* approach to communication regardless of whether the information is appreciated or desired. It's the process equivalent of *"tell them anyway, that way they can't say they haven't been told…"*

In our minimalistic process design approach, we should be viewing our passive Inform parties through the lens of *PULL* information - i.e. how can they get the information of process status when/if they want it.

There are several routes to achieve this: Manager portals, dashboards, reports, etc. and I believe we are best served by thinking of our processes as being like online shipment tracking - i.e. where's the package right now, and when is it likely to be delivered? In such a model I can quickly access information pertinent to me, and that I can act upon (e.g. making sure I'm at home to sign for the delivery, etc.)

To summarize, the root cause of this RACI challenge is that we have long history of over-involving stakeholders from within the HR function and from the business itself. Design your process to involve only appropriate stakeholders and then manage the resulting change in expectations caused by your design.

And, with that, we're done!

Phew, we've come a long way since we first identified that someone wanted to get something done, haven't we?

Pat yourself on the back for staying the course. The good news is that the majority of our structural work is done. Of course, that doesn't mean plain-sailing from here on out - in fact, what happens next based on our initial process design is where the game gets interesting and, if we let it, very tough indeed!

But before we heading into the next chapter, let's summarize what we've achieved here, and wrap it all together into one of our key tools: *the Process Pack*.

First of all, because it bears repeating, our definition of a process:

> ## A PROCESS IS A CONSISTENT, REPEATABLE SERIES OF STEPS TOWARDS A CLEARLY-DEFINED END-POINT

Towards this intent, in this chapter, we've fleshed out our process with:

- Specific **Start-** and **End-points**
- **Critical Success Factors** - A small number of performance measures that indicate the process has been fully completed for key stakeholder(s)
- **Key Assumptions** - Factors or conditions that must be in place external to the steps detailed in the process

- The specific steps that take place within the process - **Information**, **Actions**, **Decisions** and how they flow into each other, in either linear or parallel sequences

- **Roles** associated with each step - represented by the swim-lanes on our process charts

- A **Narrative** description of the process, providing specific clarification of each step including, where available, specific measures of step efficiency/effectiveness

- How each role is associated with each step - using Responsible, Accountable, Consulted, Informed (**RACI**)

With each of these sections complete, we have the full design of our process. And, even as you were reading that list, I hope you were feeling how the structure lines up with a template for process design… Because it does!

Take a look at the headings for my template on the next page, and feel free to swing by the tools section of hrprojmgmt.com to download your free template for this Process Pack, because you're going to use it… A lot!

PROCESS PACK

- **Process Overview**

    - Process Summary

    - Process Trigger

    - Process Completion

- **Key Assumptions**

- **Critical Success Factors**

- **Process Flow**

- **Process Narrative**

- **Process RACI**

REFINING THE PROCESS

As I mentioned at the end of the last chapter, in many ways our work is only just beginning, even though we've done a lot of the heavy-lifting of process design.

You see, the trick to building healthy, fit-for-purpose processes in HR lies not in their basic design - after all, anyone can go into a black-box room and draft a pristine optimal process - but instead in how we refine them to work in the real world.

Much of the criticism leveled at HR that we discussed way back at the start of this book is a perception that we are disconnected from what's actually happening, an ivory-tower function, bureaucratic and unhelpful. When we implement processes that don't take account of the day-to-day - both in the wider business AND in HR - then we radically decrease the likelihood of success, and of our process being DOA.

Savvy HR process designers don't wait for post-implementation continuous improvement to resuscitate the victim, they start that ball rolling before the process goes live.

In this chapter, we're going to look at four main ways in which we prepare our process for success:

- Subject Matter Expert input and pressure-testing
- Functional Intersections & Dependencies
- Exception handling

Let's dive in.

Subject Matter Experts

Earlier in the book I made the case to limit involvement in the core team - for me, one of the critical success factors for solid HR process design.

When we choose to extend our core team's reach by involvement of Subject Matter Experts (SMEs) in iterative process refinement, we flip that notion on its head, actively seeking input and opinion. The aim here is to move through versions of the draft process that bring in the wisdom of those out there in the real world.

Before we go any further, let's clearly define the role of a Subject Matter Expert:

> A SUBJECT MATTER EXPERT PROVIDES
> INPUT TO, AND FEEDBACK UPON,
> PROCESS DESIGN

It's really important to note here that the Subject Matter Expert does not have formal decision making authority in the process design - there are no veto powers here; we are not seeking permission.

In pure RACI terms, when it comes to the process design, an SME is Consulted and Informed, the Process Design Team remains Responsible and, yes, the Sponsor is Accountable.

So, given that your SMEs will help you refine your process, who should you choose, and why?

Let's take a look strategically and tactically at two factors:

1. Who has knowledge and/or experience that can help inform our process design?
2. Who represents a faction of stakeholders who will be affected by our process design?

Obviously, there may be SMEs that span both of these factors, however that doesn't present any unique challenges other than being a double-whammy!

Process SMEs

When we design a process in the abstract - i.e. away from where the rubber is already hitting the road - it's easy to make assumptions about what will work or not, and what is feasible in the day-to-day. This is a hazard of breaking things down into simple, movable shapes on a process flow.

Challenging these assumptions is where process SMEs can add real value to our design.

Our Process SMEs are qualified simply because they know how the current process does, and doesn't, work. So, typically these will be the current process owners or experts.

We may also include external expert SMEs - for example, if we are implementing an aspect of HRIS that requires or triggers an ancillary process, we may include a rep from the HRIS product team. That said, such involvement veers closer to Functional Intersections/Dependencies that we're going to talk about later in this chapter.

The primary involvement of Process SMEs is to provide specific knowledge or experience - I like to think that they are the people who can best fill out the specific step descriptions of the process narrative - i.e. *"When we say this step happens, what actually happens?"*

In fact, this knowledge can be really useful in testing whether we have the right step, or if we're missing sub-routines.

Let's go back to our example process for a moment:

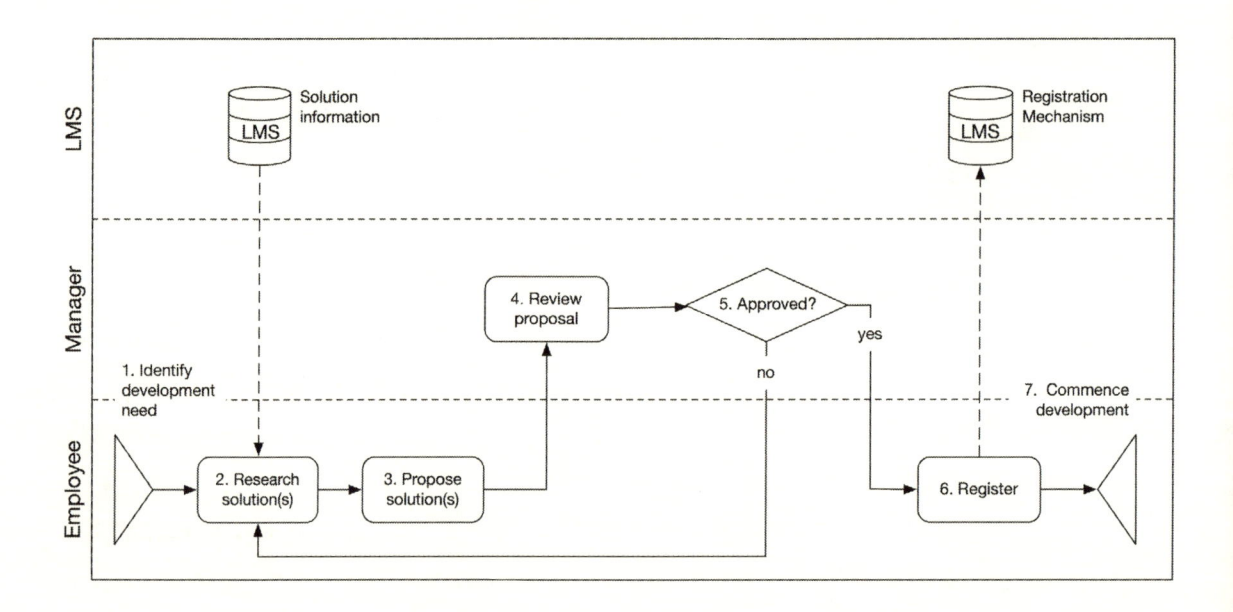

ID	Stakeholder	Step	Description
1	Employee	Identify learning need	Employee identifies a learning need - this may occur during the normal course of working or (e.g.) as part of a developmental review.
2	Employee	Research solution(s)	Employee researches possible learning solutions within the Learning Management System, as well as external alternatives.
3	Employee	Propose solution(s)	Employee completes a learning proposal template and uses online work-flow to submit for Manager review.
4	Manager	Review proposal	Manager reviews learning proposal for fit with employee development aims, business objectives, time availability and budget.
5	Manager	Approved (Y/N)	Y - Manager communicates approval to Employee N - Manager communicates non-approval to Employee and agrees next step - either refreshed proposal or no learning option will be approved
6	Employee	Register	Employee registers for approved learning solution(s) using Learning Management System registration, or external sign-up (as appropriate)

In particular let's imagine that we're running this past an L&D course administrator to see if we've missed anything.

They may point out that it all looks fine but that in step 4, the manager would have to ensure they had training budget for the individual employee, so would have to consult Finance. At minimum, this adds an extra role to the process with a Finance role having **C** on our RACI (even if we do not add a swim lane to the flow).

They may also note that when the employee reaches step 6, if the learning intervention is a standardized course, L&D would have a to decide which of a bank of providers is selected as provider. As this would appear to be a manual process, we could probably handle in the narrative itself rather than provide a separate role/step. Why so? Because earlier in our process design, we decided to sweep all of the L&D implications into a single swim-lane. In this case, we are identifying a Functional Intersection/Dependency which our process assumes is in place as part of the learning registration mechanism.

Our L&D SME may also take one look at this process and say that in step 2, the LMS is geared to create a draft learning proposal, which will feed forward to the manager dashboard and final registration. This may also be able to pull employee goals from the HRIS' performance management system as well the employee's development plan.

Bottom line, while the core team can design a simple, vanilla process, SMEs can provide the real world input that brings it to life - either to constrain the art of the doable, or inform changes that need to happen beyond the process itself. We'll talk about that a little later in the chapter.

Before we move on to Stakeholder SMEs, though, I want to take a moment to review the last page - go back and read it again if you like, I'm about to make a really important point!

Does it feel like the L&D SME is actually wanting to refine the process or, instead, justify their own role and/or involvement? Depending on the SME involved, it may be one, the other or, more likely, a mixture of both. I point this out not to slam my L&D colleagues - this is, after all, just an example process - but instead to illustrate that you have to guard against SMEs proposing process changes/details that will not serve fit-for-purpose outcomes.

Earlier in the book, I mentioned that I'm not a fan of creating process steps that are actually part of people just doing their job, this is how such steps get recommended. And, through this example, you can see how a Key Assumption (*Development solution(s) are available*) has guarded against process bloat.

Of course, this is a simple example, and I'm using it as an illustration. In real life, it's highly unlikely that you'll be able to predict every challenge that may come from process SMEs - this is one of the reasons we keep things fuzzy early on. Don't be afraid to add/refine Key Assumptions to take account of new data.

Stakeholder SMEs

Our second group of SMEs are those who represent, either formally or informally, factions who will use the process and/or who will be impacted by any change in the process.

For HR, the engagement of Stakeholder SMEs is, I believe, the *"secret sauce"* of successful implementation. As we discussed at the very outset of the book, wide opinion of HR processes is not positive - with our function described as being out-of-touch and locked in its ivory tower.

Primarily, I think this rests upon the notion that HR processes are *"done unto"* the business. Historically, the involvement of stakeholders was left to the change management and communications plan, if one even existed, post-design. And, while that is still absolutely the right place for the majority of discussion, I find it's not enough.

Involving stakeholder SMEs earlier in the process design, to pressure-test steps and provide context for how the process will work in reality, can prove extraordinarily powerful.

We'll be talking about how to involve stakeholders a little later in the book - for now, let's take a look at two types of Stakeholder SMEs that are invaluable to successful process design and implementation.

HR Business Partners

In most sizable HR functions, processes are largely owned by specialists functions, or COEs (Centers of Expertise) - e.g. the comp cycle is owned by the Rewards COE, recruiting process by Talent Acquisition, etc.

Quite often, the process and/or specialists associated with it are working directly with employees, managers and executives. However, when the process breaks in a specific area of the business, quite often it will be the appropriate HR Business Partner who hears about it first, and who is tasked with fixing things by the lead clients.

As an aside, this dynamic is the basis for what can become significant toxicity in our function and teams, but that is truly the subject of a different book!

When we draw HR Business Partners into our process design as SMEs, we are able to draw upon their unique perspective over how HR processes already land in the business. This provides opportunity to gauge the context for our process design, the changes it will cause, the likely reaction, and how to make it easier to get things done. As always we should monitor for our core resistances, but fore-warned is fore-armed.

People Managers

Let's take a look at our sample process:

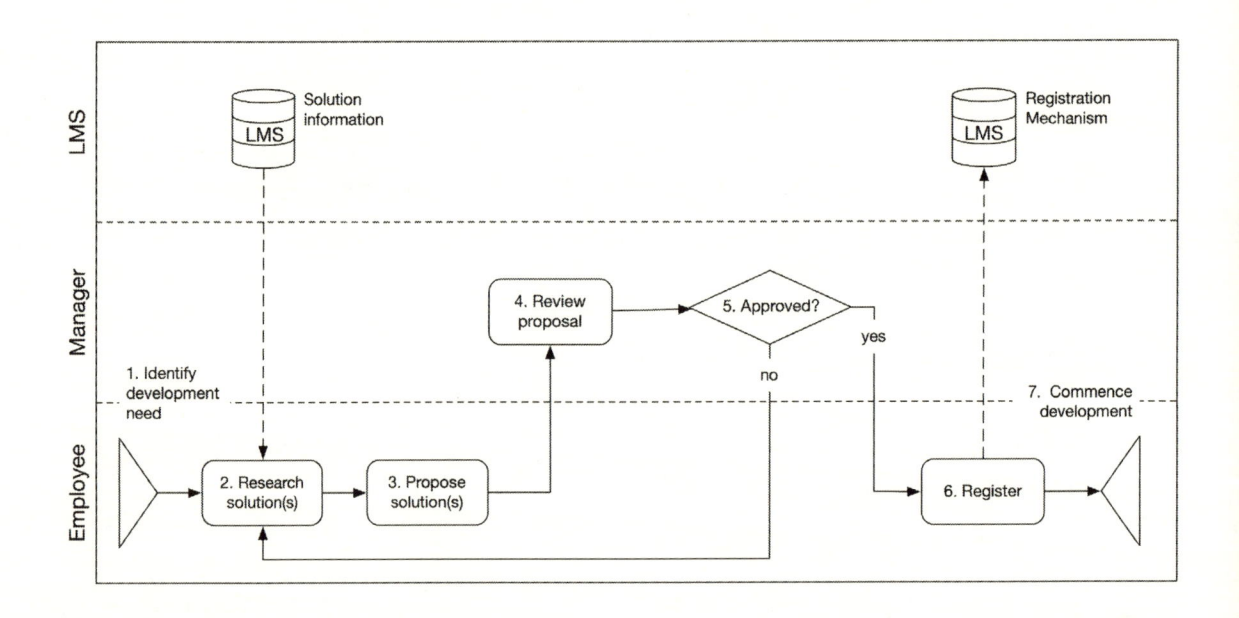

Hopefully, it should be very clear that the Manager holds a pivotal role - said simply, the process breaks if they are unable to make an approval decision.

Imagine the first time a Manager heard about this process was when it launched and they learned that they were suddenly on the hook for making that decision. It may be a little late to then find out that their department doesn't have training budgets assigned to individual employees, or that there has been an executive edict blocking all training activity for the remainder of the year, or that there is a training administrator running a shadow LMS (probably in Excel) under the department head.

While I have opinions about the appropriateness of each of these example circumstances, the fact is that involving a representative sample of managers earlier in the process design would have increased the likelihood that we could have caught issues early enough in our design that we could something about them.

If we want fit-for-purpose, minimal-bureaucracy processes, involving managers as SMEs in the design process can be the game-changer.

To summarize, we have talked about two groups of SMEs. The first are Process SMEs, those people who have knowledge/experience of the process in question. The second are stakeholder SMEs, in the main these are either HR Business Partners or Managers, and they have knowledge/experience of context in which the process occurs.

When we involve SMEs we extend the reach of our process design and access real-world, lived wisdom. This is extraordinarily powerful in refining our process to be truly fit-for-purpose. And, as we'll see later on, we also gain an advantage during implementation thanks to our involvement strategy.

With that said, let's take a look at Functional Intersections & Dependencies.

Case Study: Subject Matter Experts

To best illustrate how SMEs can be involved in process design, let's travel back to 2002, when a much younger version of me (with significantly more hair), was asked to lead a global process alignment project for the global R&D HR function in support of what, at the time, was the single largest merger in the pharmaceutical industry.

The aim of the project was simple, align all transactional HR processes (grouped into 9 process *"families"*) to facilitate the global corporate implementation of the PeopleSoft platform. And, though the aim was simple, the complexity was not! Through the merger, R&D HR had doubled in size, from 2 physical locations to 5, from around 80 HR colleagues to nearly 150. Each site had its own manual process, systems and norms.

We had a year, and I would lead the project from our UK site in Sandwich, Kent - though I often joked that I did most of my work in Heathrow departure lounge!

From the outset, our approach was to involve rather than isolate - I was certain that, when we finally got to implementation, having *"someone I know"* involved in the project would reap dividends.

As a result, my small core team were US-based, from multiple sites, and equally split between HR business partners and COE specialists, along with consulting support. Wider than the core team, however, it was our involvement of SMEs that really led to the lasting success of the project. For each process *"family"* we asked in-scope sites to nominate an HR SME.

While this was sometimes an HR business partner, sometimes a COE specialist, their remit was clear. Feed current practice to the core team, and then participate in an iterative refinement of the aligned process to pressure test implications for implementation and impact. Our SMEs were our feedback loop to the wider HR community, and partners in our design process, and we encouraged them to actively pursue discussions throughout the project.

Fast forward a little while, and we're launching the full suite of aligned processes at our next Global R&D HR meeting. As I presented the introductory session, I asked everyone involved in the project to stand - fully 30% of the room did so.

By design, we had enabled the HR function to say *"we did this!"*

Functional Intersections & Dependencies

Our Subject Matter Experts provide very human context to our process design, helping us understand the current state, and pressure-test the implications.

If we were to stop at SME input, though we would be destined to fail, simply because:

EVERY PIECE OF HR'S WORK CONNECTS TO SOMETHING ELSE

I'd best pause to let you read that again because, if you can't tell from my tone of voice, it's *really important*.

While there's a much wider discussion to be had about HR and ivory towers (whether real or perceived) let's stick closer to home and talk about process.

Simply put, no process exists in a vacuum.

We've already looked at this a little bit via RACI charting and, even in our simple example process, and our discussion of SMEs, we've seen the connection to systems (e.g. LMS), organizations (e.g. L&D), Stakeholders (e.g. external vendors), Governance (e.g. managerial decision making and budget), and the list goes on…

In fact, like a game of *"Six Degrees of Kevin Bacon"*, we can theoretically connect any process to practically anything happening in the organization. That's not the best idea, and not really much fun, except maybe as a subtle delaying/avoidance tactic akin to those we discussed earlier in the book.

Instead, let's practice the art of the doable and take a more structured approach to the ecosystem within which the process exists.

We'll do this by examining two broad factors: *Functional Intersections*, and *Dependencies*.

Functional Intersections

Put simply, for our scenario, a functional intersection occurs when an HR process touches a process owned by another function.

The most obvious example to illustrate this would be in the new employee onboarding process, where the new employee might need to receive a security badge, office key, a lap-top and/or cell-phone, etc.

In the majority of circumstances, it is unlikely that HR is on the hook to make those things happen - though I do note that in some smaller companies, I have seen some odd functions placed under HR's control - so the process requires something from other functions, or specialists, such as Security, IT, Facilities Management, etc.

In this example, the ancillary functions act as SUPPLIERS to the onboarding process, however it's also important to note that they, and other functions, may be downstream CUSTOMERS of our process.

For example, as part of onboarding, the CEO may have a regular round-table with new starters, and our onboarding process may need to let their office know the who and when of the start date.

In our onboarding process flow, we might consider indicating these ancillary processes with a different symbol and swim-lane, however this can quickly make our process flow heavy and overly complex.

In our onboarding example, we could end up with swim-lanes for Security, Facilities, IT, CEO Office, etc. This becomes another case of scope creep, where we end up trying to map *everything everywhere* that is connected to our process. Hopefully you can see that this can end up an exercise in madness?!!

In our earlier example of the learning need, we actually have a Functional Intersection in the form of the LMS, which is managed by the L&D function - we also discussed this in the SME section - and, again, our process doesn't attempt to map how the LMS works or is structured, it simply indicates an input at step 2 and an output at step 6:

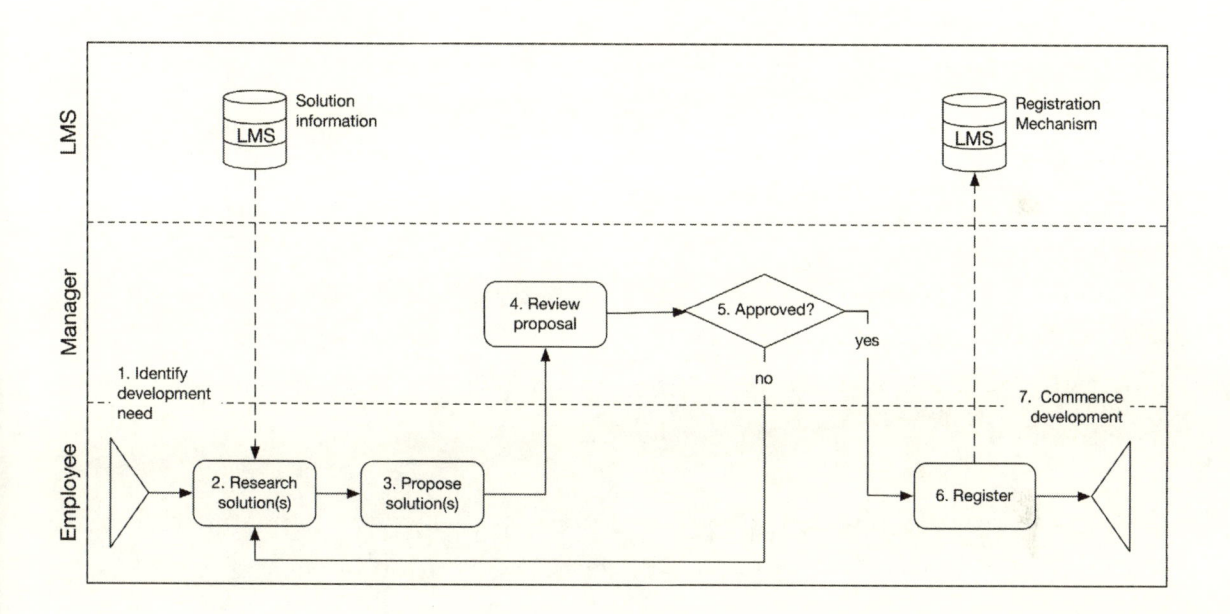

To summarize:

A FUNCTIONAL INTERSECTION HAPPENS WHEN A PROCESS SOMEWHERE ELSE IN THE COMPANY DOES SOMETHING DIRECTLY RELATED TO OUR PROCESS…

Either because we need them to do it in order to make our process successful…

Or because they can't do it without our process informing/enabling/triggering their action.

Hopefully, it's becoming clear that you should think simply in terms of INPUTS and OUTPUTS of our process - said differently, our process RECEIVES something, or it PROVIDES something. And we capture the specifics of each transfer in our process pack.

Increasingly, though not exclusively, Functional Intersections happen in the SAAS cloud or data warehouses, and are a matter of information flows and cross-system look-ups.

For this reason, I'm a strong proponent that any sizable process design project in HR should include a representative from the IT function, at minimum as an SME but preferably as a full team-member - in my earlier case study, our consulting partners played this role as experts in the PeopleSoft architecture.

Dependencies

Our process has a dependency when it relies on something being in place or happening. Now, if that sounds a lot like the Functional Intersections we just discussed, it's because there are certainly some overlaps/grey areas.

For me, the difference comes down to the nature of the connection: PASSIVE vs. ACTIVE.

Our description of Functional Intersections is active - i.e. we cause something to happen, or respond to something happening. For dependencies, we assume something is already in place and ready to go - i.e. it's passively waiting for us to call.

Let's revisit our learning need example to show how a dependency plays out:

ID	Stakeholder	Step	Description
1	Employee	Identify learning need	Employee identifies a learning need - this may occur during the normal course of working or (e.g.) as part of a developmental review.
2	Employee	Research solution(s)	Employee researches possible learning solutions within the Learning Management System, as well as external alternatives.
3	Employee	Propose solution(s)	Employee completes a learning proposal template and uses online work-flow to submit for Manager review.
4	Manager	Review proposal	Manager reviews learning proposal for fit with employee development aims, business objectives, time availability and budget.
5	Manager	Approved (Y/N)	Y - Manager communicates approval to Employee N - Manager communicates non-approval to Employee and agrees next step - either refreshed proposal or no learning option will be approved
6	Employee	Register	Employee registers for approved learning solution(s) using Learning Management System registration, or external sign-up (as appropriate)

Specifically, let's look at step 2, where the employee (RA) researches potential learning solutions.

We already have a Functional Intersection to the L&D Function via the LMS. And, if you remember, we have a big key assumption that: *Development solution(s) are available*.

Our dependency here is that the information about the development solutions is available in the LMS, is appropriate to the employee's situation, and aids decision-making.

Going deeper, let's say the company has a job library, based around competencies, we might expect that the development solutions in the LMS are categorized by that library and provide support for competency-based learning decisions.

Dependencies are really more granular assumptions and, as such, don't float up to the lofty-heights of being designated a Key Assumption.

In our example, if no development solutions are available then the process breaks, hence it being a Key Assumption. However, if the information in the LMS is incomplete, half-baked or even completely inaccurate, the employee can still propose a learning solution - i.e. the process doesn't break.

Now, there's a BIG clue as to a longer-term opportunity in that last paragraph - did you spot it?

> WHEN WE THINK OF CONTINUOUS IMPROVEMENT OF PROCESS, IT IS OFTEN OUR DEPENDENCIES THAT PRESENT LEVERAGE POINTS

In our example, there can be little doubt that the better step 2 goes, the easier the rest of the process flows, and the greater the likelihood of a positive learning outcome. Said differently, to enable employees to best learn what they need to learn, we are dependent on a high-quality curriculum being available for review on the LMS.

Exception Handling

Earlier in the book, we discussed a form of resistance I called *Boiling The Ocean* - this happens when a resistant stakeholder attempts to slow down the proposed process design by throwing in additional, ancillary processes that could benefit from redesign.

In this section, we're going to look at possible exceptions to our process and how to handle them during the design phase - if we're not careful, these can quickly become a close cousin of *Boiling The Ocean* - we might think of chasing possible exceptions as an exercise in *death-by-sub-division*.

Protecting against this is all a matter of blue socks.

Before we get to that, though, let's start with a definition:

> AN EXCEPTION OCCURS WHEN A SITUATION DEMANDS THAT THE PROCESS DOES NOT OPERATE AS DESIGNED

Let's pick this apart to make sure we're clear on some important distinctions.

First of all, an exception is situational - i.e. it happens in real-time, while the process is running.

And, when this situation presents itself, the process as designed BREAKS. It's really important to understand this when it comes to legislating for exceptions.

It may seem redundant to say it this way but, if the process doesn't break, then it works. Now, it may not work well, it may not be optimal, and it may not deliver the full set of outcomes for which it was designed. But it works.

In such a case, we are NOT designing for an exception, we are ensuring our process is robust.

For example, our benefits enrollment process may have separate requirements for hourly workers than for salaried workers. In our process design, we may handle this as separate pathways or, more likely, by ensuring the dependencies (external to the process) of benefits information and mechanisms are clear and navigable - once again, this is an example of designing a minimal process.

To summarize, it is possible for a process to have a different *"flavor"* for different participants, however we should aim for our process to be as singular as possible, with variance handled via dependency and/or functional intersection.

Even when we design with this intent and approach, we inevitably end up playing the *Exception Game*, a form of resistance that will assuredly rear its head during your process refinement sessions and, if not handled properly, has a high likelihood of grinding things to a halt.

The *Exception Game* is a version of *"but what if…"* played by SMEs, and is a theoretical search for things that could break the process. In this imaginary landscape, every step is challenged for how it would work if <participant A> was <situationally challenged> in some way.

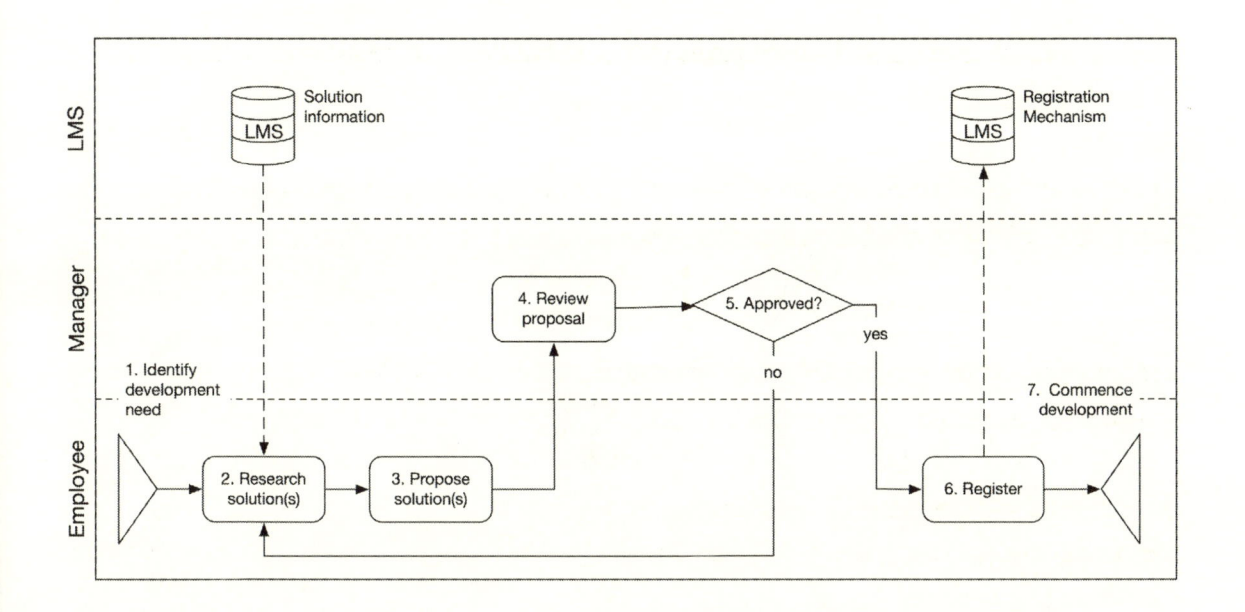

[Process flow diagram showing swim lanes for LMS, Manager, and Employee with steps: 1. Identify development need, 2. Research solution(s), 3. Propose solution(s), 4. Review proposal, 5. Approved?, 6. Register, 7. Commence development. LMS databases shown for Solution information and Registration Mechanism.]

Now, as we've discussed, it is possible for processes to break, in which case planning for exception handling is appropriate, but that's not what this game is about - it's about the search for the impossible exception... for each step... requiring debate of all possibilities...

Well, you can see how it would slow down the design work, right?

Let's take a look at a specific case using our learning example:

Now, imagine you're in a process refinement session with a small number of SMEs and one of them asks: *"but how does this work for an employee who's on a corrective performance plan?"*

That's a reasonable potential situation to raise, and so we have to consider whether the process would break.

Take a look at the process flow... Will it break if the employee is on a corrective performance plan?

The simple answer is: *No*. In fact, there's a strong chance that step 1 (*Identify a learning need*) may be directly driven by the performance plan!

That said, there is some nuance here. If, due to the performance plan, there is no hope of the Manager approving the proposed learning solution, then steps 2, 3 and 4 are a waste of time and effort. And steps 6 and 7 never happen.

That sounds pretty much like a broken process, right?

Well, it is but that doesn't mean we have to design for this exception.

Remember we already have a Key Assumption for this process is that: *Development solutions are available*.

In this exception, we're saying that this Key Assumption is not met for employees on performance plans. This could be due to company-wide policy, it could be local departmental practices, it could be budgetary constraint…

Whatever *"could be"* it is, though, my opinion is that we don't need to design the process to include it in terms of additional steps. Instead, I would include a dependency in step 2 (*Research solution(s)*) for clear guidance - policy or otherwise - on whether the employee is eligible for learning solutions.

Alternatively, from a more empowered viewpoint, why should HR legislate what an employee does or does not research, or what proposal they may choose to present to their Manager? That sounds like old school bureaucratic thinking, doesn't it?

In our empowered view, the Manager has approval at step 5, and that's enough.

And, if you check the process narrative, you'll find we've covered it in the *N* clause:

ID	Stakeholder	Step	Description
5	Manager	Approved (Y/N)	N - Manager communicates non-approval to Employee and agrees next step - either refreshed proposal or no learning option will be approved
			Y - Manager communicates approval to Employee

"But what happens if the Manager makes the wrong decision, Vince?!!"

They may well do. But that's not the purview of our process.

Just in case you'd forgotten, earlier in the book we agreed a significant guiding principle:

DO NOT REPLACE ACCOUNTABILITY WITH PROCESS STEPS

Once again, we're at the crux of the purpose of HR processes (*to help people get things done*) vs. the old-school view of the function (*to protect against risk and bad things happening*).

If a Manager doesn't know how to make a good decision on learning solutions, then that is an issue of capability, accountability and/or information. Our process can really only touch one of those things (*information*).

Adjusting the process for *everyone*, in order to protect against a *minority of people* who might do it wrong is a serious *RED FLAG*.

This is because, in essence, we're saying that the exception should be treated as if it is the norm; which is right back to the old days of no process whatsoever.

When I encounter this red flag, I always look at where capability, accountability and information are in question, and make sure my Key Assumptions, Dependencies and Functional Intersections are in place to catch the exception.

A really good example of protecting against the few by legislating the many happens during the typical performance management cycle, where templates and deadlines force compliance, supposedly to drive equal treatment across the employee population. Except… Low capability managers aren't made better by the process, and Strong managers are actually slowed down, hobbled by the process. And yes, average managers remain average regardless of process. Bottom line for the performance management process: hire and develop good to great managers, and manage the performance of weaker managers. Neither of which sounds like the performance management process we have in place!

We've gone quite deep on what was truly meant as an illustrative example, but I chose to do so because it's indicative of how quickly the *Exception Game* can spin up deep and wide discussion, all of which delay or even stall the process design.

Remember, all of this discussion was spun up by one potential exception (if the employee was on a performance plan). But did you notice how one exception gave birth to the next (manager capability to make decision)?

In the Exception Game, that's just how discussion go, with one exception branching out to other exception, proliferating ever more widely until it seems there's no hope for a single process design.

While some amount of pressure testing is healthy, being able to catch the downward spiral early is a critical competency during process refinement.

And this is where blue socks can help.

Introducing the "Blue Sock Clause"!

Design enough processes and, sooner or later, you're going to end up in a room with one or more HR SMEs who insist that seemingly every step of the process in question needs to be customized for each individual employee.

These HR SMEs are playing the Exception Game at its highest level, making each potential exception sound worthy of consideration.

And, while any potential exception may result in a formal exception in your final process, the energy, time and resources spent debating and deciding that can become overwhelming.

Make no mistake, no matter how well intentioned, this is a resistance play - seeking to slow down, or stall the inevitable change that a redesigned process will cause.

This resistance can range from simple curiosity through to willful sabotage, and sometimes, the latter is dressed up as the former.

Either way, the resistance finds its voice in the form of a question along the lines of: *"How does this step work for…"*

I follow the rule of 3 strikes here for each SME, making a mental note of how often their knee jerk is to raise potential exceptions, and this question framing is my indicator.

Listen to the debate of this first potential exception, let the team discuss the whys and wherefores, and if it turns out to not be an exception pretty obviously, make a mental note (you may actually want to track these in a reference document for the team while you're learning to play this particular game).

Let the cycle run and, once again, capture any obvious non-exceptions.

As you listen to the discussions, you'll begin to notice when the debate is for debate's sake, with little substance to the exception in question; you'll catch the stalling tactic in action.

And here, at 3rd strike, with an understanding smile on your face, is where you interrupt the conversation and ask: *"Aren't we really asking how this step works if the person is wearing blue socks?"*

Believe me, this pattern interrupt has an amazing effect upon such discussions. You will immediately see confusion - and that's a good thing. Depending on the HR SME in question you might experience bluster or raised voices - again, a good thing.

I can't stress enough how you have to practice a light touch when you deploy the Blue Sock Clause.

You see, what we're aiming to do here is undermine a resistance without attacking the person. We're using humor/satire to defuse a land-mine, not making the SME in question feel shamed or victimized. So, light touch it is.

As we've discussed, resistance is an emotion that has found no means of expression; the blue sock clause is an honorable way to acknowledge this and, subtly, to open the door to discuss the background fear.

Practically speaking, it flips the focus of the conversation from the process design having to justify why the situation isn't an exception, to the SME having to justify why it is!

Invoking the *"Blue Sock Clause"* is a light-hearted, non-confrontational way to burst the bubble (or ego) of the SME in question.

In fact, the first few times I used it, the team burst into laughter, because everyone in HR has experienced (and, I would argue, participated in) this form of resistance at some point.

Sometimes, invoking the *"Blue Sock Clause"* has deeper benefit.

You see, in design sessions with multiple SMEs, the majority will often be growing increasingly frustrated with a lone hold-out who continues to play the game, they'll be ready to move on but feel powerless to change the person's behavior. As the process design lead, you have authority to push though any way you choose, but by asking about blue socks, you're able to gently steer the work towards resolution, leaving the majority with the knowledge that they've been heard and respected.

In my experience, over time, core team members increasingly called resistant behaviors early using the *"Blue Sock Clause"*; and I heard multiple times, both directly and indirectly, that the term had gained traction outside the process design project; that members of HR were using it to challenge their own work, that of their colleagues and their interaction with business clients!

Bottom line, if you're facing death by exception, you could do worse than searching out some blue socks!

One final, practical note

We've already talked about our process pack, and how it forms the core working document for your process design. If you're leading any sizable effort, there will be a lot of back-and-forth of this document, which will go through several iterations.

Indeed, when I was leading the global process alignment project I described earlier, it was not uncommon for the team to be video-conferencing in from multiple locations, with simultaneous editing of the latest draft by the whole team. This draft would then be circulated to SMEs for offline edits, which we would then circle back to the core team to generate next draft. Rinse and repeat.

Now, we were doing this long before online collaborative workspace such as Google Docs, etc. existed, but that only makes it easier for you to take what I've presented in the book and bring it to life in your process design efforts.

What the technology can't give you, however, is a commitment to working in a structured way.

During the design and refinement process, there can be many moving pieces, and I've found that the only way to stay sane is to use document version control (I include this in all my templates) and centralized document repositories. Please, please, please do not rely on your email inbox and folders as storage for process design iterations - it's a recipe for disaster!

Later in the book, we're going to talk about formal Change Control approaches once the process is live, and the work you do here to structure document history and storage provides an early opportunity to prepare the ground.

At minimum, your working history provides a full reference for decisions and choices made in the original design, as well as each draft version of the process pack right through to the final endorsed release.

HR doesn't have a great reputation for technology efficiency or effectiveness, or even for structured, planful working practices. That may not be you and, if so, congratulations, but if it's anywhere near close to your truth, make sure you learn quick and well how to make structured working support your efforts.

Enough said for now, we'll circle back to this subject a little when we cover Change Control.

TOWARDS IMPLEMENTATION

As we start this chapter, I want to be very clear in setting expectations. I'm not including detailed approaches for implementation and/or change management here. Frankly, both topics deserve their own book AND draw from disciplines far removed from process design itself.

What we're about to discuss are the key points and highlights that relate to implementation. An easy way to think about this is that we're going to be covering *"feed-forward"* to implementation from our process design work - you'll see I use that term a lot.

If the feed-forward doesn't work for you though, think of it as the inputs our process design must provide to the implementation team.

I like to think of our *feed-forward* as consisting of two parts:

- People
- Process

People

Who does the process affect?

We're going to keep things very simple here and look at two classes of people who will experience changes in relation to our process: *Targets* and *Supporters*. Once again, don't get hung up on terminology, it's more important to grasp the concepts beyond the words.

Targets

Put simply a Target of your process design is someone who will use, or be impacted directly by the process. And yes, if we're playing the cute HR resistance game of *Boiling The Ocean* we can theoretically draw a line from our process to any individual on the planet; but we're not those playing games, are we?!

For our purposes, think of a process target as anyone who has a Responsible (**R**) or Accountable (**A**) on our RACI chart.

Let's take a look at our example RACI:

ID	Step	Employee	Manager	LMS
1	Identify learning need	RA	C	
2	Research solution(s)	RA		C
3	Propose solution(s)	RA	I	
4	Review proposal	C	RA	C
5	Approved (Y/N)	I	RA	

ID	Step	Employee	Manager	LMS
6	Register	RA		CI

Clearly, the targets of this process are the Employee and the Manager, and thanks to RACI we can see clearly exactly how our process affects them.

Supporters

Our example process is lighter on supporters - those people consulted (C) or informed (I) on the RACI. Technically we only have the LMS defined. Remember though that we touched on Functional Intersections & Dependencies in the last chapter, specifically:

"Our dependency here is that the information about the development solutions is available in the LMS, is appropriate to the employee's situation, and aids decision-making.

Going deeper, let's say the company has a job library, based around competencies, we might expect that the development solutions in the LMS are categorized by that library and provide support for competency-based learning decisions."

So, though the RACI doesn't delineate it as a process step, we should include L&D in our *feed-forward* as a Supporter to the process - in this case the information would be provided by our Dependencies and Functional Intersections capture.

Who can help?

Wrapped around the process design, however, are another group of people who we can *feed-forward* to the change efforts: *Sponsor*, *Core Team*, and *SMEs*.

Sponsor

We touched on the role of the Sponsor in process implementation back in **Chapter 3: Laying The Groundwork** - if you haven't taken that content to heart yet, make sure you go back and read it again (there's a reason why I describe the Sponsor as a critical role!)

Core Team

Even if the Core Team was assembled solely for the process design work and subsequently disbanded, they can acts as advocates and deep-dive resources for the change management effort.

SMEs

When it comes to implementation, SMEs are the secret weapon of process design. Their involvement in the design process gives them co-ownership of success and, as a result, they can be powerful ambassadors for the new process, advocating for change and explaining how decisions were reached along the way. In a very real sense, SMEs are the human face of process design, so add them as available resources in the *feed-forward* to implementation.

In my case study in the last chapter, I mentioned that 30% of HR had been involved directly in the process design effort. When we reached implementation, that involvement provided a reservoir of trust and insight that we couldn't have achieved in any other way without significant resource expenditure. Bottom line: don't underestimate the power of engaged SMEs!

Now that we've covered people, let's look at the process itself.

Translating your process pack

So, we know who is affected by the process, now we need to *feed-forward* how they are affected by the process.

During implementation, there will undoubtedly be a need for at least some, if not all, of the following:

- Elevator speech
- From -> To detail
- Training Material
- Frequently Asked Questions
- Online Help
- Briefing Packs
- Communications

(And the list goes on… Which is precisely why we're not covering change management in detail in this book!)

The good news is that you've already done all the hard work to be able to provide source material for all of the above; it's all in your Process Pack.

Let's take a look at a couple of examples to illustrate how you can use your content. We'll start with extracting the foundation of an Elevator Speech.

Just to review, the concept of an elevator speech is to be able to simply describe a topic in the time you might share a ride in an elevator - mostly 30 seconds (though, when I lived and worked in NYC, it was often much longer than that!) Put simply, an Elevator speech is the shortest meaningful story you can tell about your process.

To generate the Elevator Speech for this process, we'll go back to our narrative:

ID	Stakeholder	Step	Description
1	Employee	Identify learning need	Employee identifies a learning need - this may occur during the normal course of working or (e.g.) as part of a developmental review.
2	Employee	Research solution(s)	Employee researches possible learning solutions within the Learning Management System, as well as external alternatives.
3	Employee	Propose solution(s)	Employee completes a learning proposal template and uses online work-flow to submit for Manager review.
4	Manager	Review proposal	Manager reviews learning proposal for fit with employee development aims, business objectives, time availability and budget.
5	Manager	Approved (Y/N)	Y - Manager communicates approval to Employee N - Manager communicates non-approval to Employee and agrees next step - either refreshed proposal or no learning option will be approved
6	Employee	Register	Employee registers for approved learning solution(s) using Learning Management System registration, or external sign-up (as appropriate)

If we look at the Employee we can boil down a simplified summary version of the process steps:

When a learning need is identified, the Employee researches options, reviews potential solutions with their Manager and, if approved, registers to attend.

I just read that out loud slowly in a little over 7 seconds.

A headline would be even quicker: *Employee registers for an approved learning solution.*

FADE IN

SFX: DING!

The elevator doors open, Vince enters to find Stakeholder. Vince hits his floor and the doors close. After a moment…

Stakeholder: So, what are you up to these days.

Vince: This and that… Helping employees learn things…

Stakeholder: Really?

Vince: Uh-huh. Putting a process in to make the approval really easy.

Stakeholder: That'll be a relief - no more forms!

Vince: No more forms!

SFX: DING!

Vince: That's my floor… Stay tuned.

Vince steps out of the Elevator.

FADE OUT

Now, as I've been at pains to remind you throughout the book, this is a simple process flow, so deriving the Elevator Speech was always going to be straightforward. But don't be fooled... Most every process can be distilled down to such an essential description. The clue is to identify the key player - think of it as the star of the movie, the lead role in the play.

You can get at this via the RACI chart:

ID	Step	Employee	Manager	LMS
1	Identify learning need	RA	C	
2	Research solution(s)	RA		C
3	Propose solution(s)	RA	I	
4	Review proposal	C	RA	C
5	Approved (Y/N)	I	RA	
6	Register	RA		CI

Even a quick scan will tell you the Employee is the main player. It's pretty obvious that the Elevator Speech would present this as an Employee-enabling process.

But, beyond the Elevator Speech, I want to use this example to highlight a really important point: *Focus is the focus!*

We started the book with two pretty-safe assumptions:

NOBODY CARES ABOUT HR PROCESSES

HR BELIEVES EVERYONE CARES ABOUT HR PROCESSES

We also shared a Guiding Principle:

DON'T MAKE THINGS MORE COMPLEX THAN THEY NEED TO BE

When it comes to implementation, HR often falls into the trap of over-communicating minutiae and missing the big picture. As we've discussed, the majority of people in any organization only care about HR processes when they need to get something done; specifically at a point a time.

We don't need people to be deep experts in every aspect of a process; nor do they want to be so.

In this case, the Employee doesn't need to know up-front how the Manager makes the decision, or how the LMS works, or how budgets are assigned, etc. There is a lot of process that just doesn't matter to the Employee, who just wants to find and begin the learning solution.

When it comes to *feeding-forward* to implementation, I like to think of any process as being like the electrical grid. If the room is getting dark, I want to turn on a light, so I walk over to a switch on the wall and press it. The light comes on, I am no longer in darkness (hurrah!) and I can go on about my business.

I didn't have to consider how the wiring in my house works, nor how the electric current arrived at my house, nor how it was generated, nor how electricity even works… I just wanted to turn on the light, so I did so.

We should aim to make HR processes as specific and simple.

"But Vince," I hear you cry, *"there'll be questions!"*

And there will be, for sure. In our example, Managers will need some guidance/ briefing on how they arrive at approval decisions. The LMS (and Learning & Development team) will need to provide appropriate information.

Simplifying the face of the process does not imply delivery isn't complex.

But that does not mean we have to force the complexity to be visible and understood by all players.

At the start of the book, we talked about *"light-touch HR"*:

"It's not easy to practice light-touch HR - we are pushing against a heavy weight of functional and organizational pressure to prove relevance, credibility and capability."

Over-communicating specifics of a process to non-interested parties is one of the ways we can fail in this intent, and a major reason that HR processes, and the function itself, are labeled as burdensome, bureaucratic and slow.

So, with our Elevator Speech covered, let's look at another example of extracting value from our process pack: *Training Materials*.

Notice here that we're not immediately assuming the process design team creates the training - that may happen if your project is scoped to include that activity, but it's not a safe assumption otherwise; it's actually an example of the HR knee-jerk we discussed earlier: *I've been asked, so I must do.*

What we can provide is an indication of what needs to be in place to make steps successful - for training that means knowledge, capability, and behavior. And, just to make the point once again, we aren't the change managers, so we don't have to work out how it gets done in implementation.

Once again, I look to the RACI chart to assess source for training materials:

ID	Step	Employee	Manager	LMS
1	Identify learning need	RA	C	
2	Research solution(s)	RA		C
3	Propose solution(s)	RA	I	
4	Review proposal	C	RA	C
5	Approved (Y/N)	I	RA	
6	Register	RA		CI

Once again, I'm looking for the R and A steps, because that's where someone is going to do or decide something. In our example, we can summarize the following by the two roles:

- Employee needs to know how to translate a learning need into research criteria, including feedback from their Manager
- Employee needs to know how to access and use the LMS
- Employee needs to know how to propose options to their Manager

- Employee needs to know how to register for learning solutions via LMS
- Manager needs to know how to review, approve and communicate decisions relating to learning solutions

That's it. Nothing more, nothing less. Now, a seasoned change management and communications expert might take that list of requirements and say that there are two major training components.

Let's handle the simple one first. Managers are always reviewing, approving and communicating decisions - it's almost the definition of management. So, in the spirit of light-touch, and assuming that managerial training is already in place, the only training needed fro our process is informational; specifically, approval criteria. If that doesn't sound like it will fall neatly into an online approval flow, then nothing does.

The second training component speaks to the Employee and, again, a seasoned change manager might well be focused on organization cultural change and colleague engagement. They would spot how the transactional aspects of the process can be wrapped in more engagement-driven module that speaks to the employee learning journey:

- *"How to grow your capabilities and career at…"*
- *"Accelerate your growth - maximize your impact…"*
- *"In brief - How the LMS helps you find the right learning solution…"*
- *"Delivering the PEOPLE value through learning…"*

And there are countless others that could have made the list - once again, that's not the focus of process design but more the marketing/training of change management and communication.

We could continue down the list of change management deliverables and how the Process Pack provides source material, but I'll save that for your experiential learning and each one is pretty much what we've laid out above, using the narrative, flow diagram and RACI chart to *feed-forward*.

Sharing the wiring

Earlier, I suggested that for our targets, we treat the process as we would a electric light-switch; easy, uncomplicated, functional. That doesn't mean that the electrical infrastructure doesn't exist.

For our process, that infrastructure resides in both the Functional Intersections & Dependencies and, subtly, in the **(C)**onsult and **(I)**nform actions of our RACI chart.

Our change management resource will ensure that the former are shared with the relevant owners, and that the paths for **C** and **I** are fully described and available.

So, we've covered how you help prepare for implementation. Assuming you have a competent change management resource who has successfully implemented everything you designed, all that's left is to take a look at what happens once your newly designed process is out in the wild.

BEYOND IMPLEMENTATION

Once your process is implemented, the process design work is formally done, and the project ready for closure. And, if that's not the case, then we need to be having a very different conversation about how project management works!

That said, we would be foolish to believe that:

a) the process will never change once we've designed it; and/or…
b) that we can simply step away and have nothing to do with the process ever again.

Actually, in my experience in HR, once you've been involved in process design, it's hard to ever lose the label of the person who knows how the process works. You become something of a living information source for the process in question.

Needless to say, the better you arm the implementation work - as we discussed in the last chapter - the less this is likely to happen. If the process runs smoothly with training and support materials that actually help people get things done, then there will be fewer speed-bumps and land-mines to pull you back into your history.

If you do find yourself dragged back in, it's likely an issue to address with your Sponsor - after all, they were the ones authorizing the process design project, and they are responsible for ensuring your role had (and still has) strong boundaries compared to how the process runs in the field.

I don't want to overstate this risk but it's important to know that it can happen, particularly if you are asked to design a process over which you do NOT have ownership. In such a case, unfortunately, I have seen the owners of the process act to sabotage the new process either willfully or through unaddressed resentment that they had not been asked to lead the design work.

Once again, this is very likely a situation you would not be able to solve in isolation, and your Sponsor should be, at minimum, consulted on how to move forward.

With that said, let's take a look at what to do when the process changes.

Change Control

As I discussed in Refining The Process, during the design and refinement process, the only way to stay sane is to use document version control for your process pack and ancillary documents; structure is your friend!

But, even if you do all that well, it's still only the foundation for process Change Control.

First, let's take a look at a definition, which I've adapted from the project management discipline:

CHANGE CONTROL IS A METHODOLOGY USED TO MANAGE ANY CHANGE REQUESTS THAT IMPACT THE BASELINE OF YOUR PROCESS...

As I said earlier, we would be foolish to believe that we design a process once and can expect it to remain unchanged forevermore - though sadly, given that we still come across processes that are little more than iterations of pre-internet paper-chases, it can sometimes seem that some HR colleagues do feel that to be the case!

That's not us though and, if we know that the process will change, we should prepare the ground for it to change well.

I recommend you think of your process in similar terms to software releases.

Thus, your first go-live version will be v1.0, and any slight adjustments made in real-time to individual steps will yield v1.1, v1.2, etc. These adjustments will be approved and tracked by the process owner; for our example process that may look something like this (I've put amendments in bold):

ID	Stakeholder	Step	Previous Description	Amended Description
2	Employee	Research solution(s)	Employee researches possible learning solutions within the Learning Management System, as well as external alternatives.	Employee researches possible learning solutions within the Learning Management System, as well as external alternatives **from approved vendors**.
4	Manager	Review proposal	Manager reviews learning proposal for fit with employee development aims, business objectives, time availability and budget.	Manager reviews learning proposal for fit with employee development aims, business objectives, time availability and budget. **NOTE: New training budget guidelines**

As we see in the example, these amendments don't fundamentally change the process - in step 2, we're simply channeling the external solutions available to only those approved via the LMS, and in step 4, we're catching the fact that Managers have some new training budget guidelines.

But what if it's a bigger deal?

Well, in this approach, any significant change in the process would result in a version change to (e.g.) v2.0, etc.

What would be significant enough to cause a version change?

There isn't a hard and fast answer, as it all depends on local and organizational agreements and expectations.

From my perspective any or all of these may be significant enough to drive a version change:

- The need to form a team or involve SMEs in order to refine the process
- A change in Responsible/Accountable of any line on the RACI chart
- The need to alter the flow of multiple process steps - including if systems are introduced to automate flows
- Legal requirement for change in process
- Sufficient individual tweaks to steps have been made that the process is growing unwieldy and/or losing efficiency/effectiveness (NOTE: this one is hard to monitor if there aren't specific performance measures)
- The number of exceptions has begun to grow unmanageable and/or raise the risk of unfair treatment

Whatever the driving reason, we have to revisit the process and redefine it to match the new circumstances. Said differently, our baseline needs to change, so its a matter of Change Control.

The steps to Change Control for a process are pretty straightforward:

- Step 1 - Gather process information
- Step 2 - Generate process flow and swim-lanes
- Step 3 - Generate RACI
- Step 4 - Identify Dependencies & Functional Intersections
- Step 5 - Authorize changes and implement

Now, take a moment to review that list of steps. Does it sound familiar? It should, because it's what we've already covered earlier in this book! A version change of a process is in fact a new process redesign project, even if it may not be as in depth as the original design work.

Essentially, once confirmed and authorized by your Sponsor, it's time to dust off the history, and revisit the design materials - however, the good news is that you probably won't need to go back to first principles and *Post-It®* notes on the wall. In many ways, Change Control design will feel much more like one of your refinement sessions, where you're responding to SME feedback, and the same guiding principles apply even though it's not a new process design.

Some quick thoughts on shadow systems

Beyond Change Control, however, there is one further area that requires monitoring, that of *"shadow systems"*. Let's start with a definition:

A SHADOW SYSTEM EXISTS OUTSIDE OF A PROCESS TO COMPENSATE FOR PROCESS INEFFICIENCIES OR INEFFECTIVENESS

A couple of things to note here.

Firstly, though the shadow system exists outside of the process, that doesn't mean it exists outside of HR. For example, in the absence of accurate, timely data, the business may track its own headcount numbers, but it may equally be the case that the HR business partner does so at the same time! This is obviously a recipe for potentially wasted/redundant effort and inaccurate data.

And that brings us to the second point; right or wrong, the shadow systems exist because the process isn't working for the owner of the shadow system. This does NOT automatically mean the process is broken; it may be an issue with the stakeholder in question. Either way, until we have a process that delivers, we simply cannot safely make the claim that the shadow system is NOT wasted/redundant effort. And the only way we can tell is by assessing the detail.

If, for example, the process is working well for 6 out of 7 departments, but one HR rep is insistent that it's not working for their clients, then the question becomes: *is there something special happening in this department that breaks/slows the process?*

Asking the question this way is the first step towards joint problem solving - much like invoking the *Blue Sock Clause,* the aim is not to castigate the owner of the shadow system, it's to uncover reality and then plan to deal with it.

Here's an example from my own past, when running a global colleague engagement survey. We kept hearing from one country that the implementation wouldn't work, and that they wanted to aggregate and disseminate responses locally. If you've ever managed a confidential survey, you'll know that maintaining strong information protection on responses is essential. While we were therefore inclined to take a hard stance, I chose to do some listening, and it became clear that, in this country operation, a significant proportion of the work-force did not have access to a computer, at home or at work, and so could not get to their results via our distribution portal! The proposed shadow system in this case was due to a local exception that broke our process! We quickly established a route to provide hard copy results to that country, thereby eliminating the need for a shadow system.

Bottom line, when we are so focused on our process design, it's easy to fall into a knee jerk response that any shadow system is a *"bad thing"* but, when we do so, we miss the opportunity to learn and, ultimately, improve the process itself.

Over the years, I've learned that the best way to handle shadow systems is to treat them as an indicator of:

a) a potential SME; and/or…

b) a potential Dependency or even Key Assumption; and/or…

c) an extra level of training/communication/involvement during the change management process

Said bluntly, the best way to fix what's broken in HR is to take seriously what people have put in place because HR is broken - and the same goes for your process!

One final note here though, which I'll classify as a call-back from change management.

When you implement a redesigned process you will inevitably bump into gatekeepers, often the keepers of shadow systems, both within HR and out in the wilds of the organization, who have justified their organizational value, and maybe even existence, due to the fact that they *"save"* executives, managers and employees from broken HR processes.

These players are likely to resist/undermine the new process regardless, so it's better to involve them in the design process up-front so that you remove one of their major resistances: *nobody told me.*

Even if you do practice an involvement strategy, you will undoubtedly bump into hold-outs, so be ready to handle the situation appropriately - even calling in your Sponsor if necessary - just don't fall into the trap of personifying the process; you are the designer not the process itself.

A final thought on process design

We spent a lot of time earlier discussing the resistances that HR has to process design; where they come from, how they manifest and how to deal with them.

It's very likely that, in the earliest stages of your process design work, as well as when you draw closer to implementation, that you may feel change is impossible. If that's the case, I encourage you to reflect on the following observation.

I'm old enough to remember going to the bank with my bank book whenever I wanted to deposit or withdraw money. I had to think about doing that and plan for bank branch visits because cash and cheques were the only way to pay for things.

Imagine my amazement when they introduced these machines that you could put a card in and get money out *whenever you wanted!*

Now fast forward a couple of decades and I'm paying for things with my iPhone and very rarely carrying cash aside from enough to pay for incidentals. I still go to the bank, but very rarely in person, more often online.

My point here is that - as with the electrical grid example I covered earlier - most processes exist below our conscious thought. Remember:

NOBODY CARES ABOUT HR PROCESSES

HR BELIEVES EVERYBODY CARES ABOUT HR PROCESSES

No-one asked me if I would like an ATM or how an ATM should work, it just appeared one day in the wall of my bank in Watford town centre. I was surprised and amazed to be able to access my money without standing in line and waiting for my book to get stamped.

When we improve HR processes using a focused design methodology such as the one I've presented in this book, we are a lot like the team designing the ATM; creating the wiring and information flow that makes things effortless for the end user.

So long as we remain true to our scope and vision, our process will improve at least one experience of getting things done with HR.

And that, plain and simple, is the North Star of process design for Human Resources.

WHAT HAPPENS NEXT?

So, we are reaching the end of this stage of our journey together, and what a ride it has been!

I do hope that you've learned something that you can apply right away and, even if not, I'll be satisfied if I have provided even one opportunity for you to check in with your own process design mindset.

As I said way up front of the book, I believe that the potential of *people*, *teams* and *organizations* is ours to unlock, and that the better able we are to get things done, the sooner we will be able to act as a force for positive change in the world.

Process Design, particularly when delivered in HR, is not a theoretical endeavor - even if we sometimes run the risk of turning it into one, by way of an avoidance tactic! In every sense, getting things done in HR is a contact sport; relying on interactions, influence and insight.

For this reason, I'd like to invite you to join me at *HRPROJMGMT.COM*, so that we may continue our journey together as you, and I, accumulate more and more real world experience of making things happen in HR.

Together, we are building a community of HR professionals who know how to get things done, and get them done well.

At the site, you'll gain FREE access to tools and templates that I've described throughout this book. They're yours and you can use them right away.

Vincent Tuckwood is an award-winning consultant and coach with a track record of delivering high-value, high-impact projects and programs in Human Resources. Known for seamlessly blending vision & strategy with on-the-ground implementation, his writing draws valuable insights and anecdotes from nearly 30 years of success.

After 2 decades with Pfizer Inc. on both sides of the Atlantic, Vince stepped out on his own in 2010, founding his own independent consultancy, View Beyond LLC:

Email: vince@viewbeyondllc.com
Web: viewbeyondllc.com

Made in United States
Troutdale, OR
01/05/2025